Modern UK Politics

John McTaggart

Published and typeset by Modernity Publishing. PO Box 14325, Burntisland, Fife KY3 0UP.

Printed and bound by Woods of Perth. www.woodsofperth.co.uk

British Library Cataloguing-in-publication Data A catalogue record for this book is available from the British Library.

Published by Modernity Publishing

ISBN 978 0 9555750 0 6
© Modernityeducation 2007

Modern UK Politics can be purchased;

Online: www.modernityeducation.co.uk
Tel: 01383 861022
Email: modernityscotland@btconnect.com

School/college purchase order: PO Box 14325, Burntisland, Fife KY3 0UP.

Bookshops:
Blackwells
53-62 South Bridge
Edinburgh
EH1 1YS
Tel: 0131 622 8222
Email: Edinburgh@blackwell.co.uk

Kay's Bookshop
390 Morningside Road
Edinburgh, EH10 5HX
Tel: 0131 447 1265

Keep up to date with UK Politics (and all the rest of your Modern Studies).

www.modernityscotland.co.uk is the place to go to keep up to date with everything in Higher Modern Studies.

The site contains advice on how to properly prepare for the Higher exam.

There is valuable advice on essay technique for Paper 1 and report writing skills for Paper 2.

In addition to this, the content of all Study Themes is updated three times per year; in the summer, just before schools come back; in January, just before the Prelims, and in April; just before the SQA exams.

Whatever Study Themes you take in Political Issues in the UK, Social Issues or International Issues, Modernityscotland will keep your knowledge right up to date.

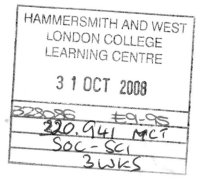

Contents

Introduction

Introduction

Modern UK Politics is intended to assist teachers and students of Higher Modern Studies. The book addresses the key content of Political Issues in the United Kingdom.

Each Section begins with "The Big Picture", which attempts to give the student an overview of the key developments in a particular Section. The Sections of *Modern UK Politics* correspond to the Study Themes of Higher Modern Studies.

While Modern Studies students will not study all of the four Sections, this does not mean that certain Sections should be ignored. There is some overlap between the Sections. Modern UK politics cannot be so easily compartmentalised!

For example, those who do Section Two, Decision Making in Central Government, may well find the content in Section One of value. Similarly, the content in Section Three, Political Parties and their Policies, will be of value to those who do any of the other Politics Sections. It may well be the source of some vital background knowledge for the Decision Making Exercise in Paper Two of Higher Modern Studies.

Throughout the book are Activities boxes to consolidate learning at school/college and at home. However, please visit www.modernityscotland.co.uk, where there is a dedicated section to Modern UK Politics. Here you will find updates on Section Content, as well as learning activities related to the Curriculum for Excellence.

Please also visit http://www.modernityeducation.co.uk/products.html, where you will find a series of podcasts related to Modern UK Politics. So, you can now access Modern Studies any time you want!

I hope you find *Modern UK Politics* of value in your Higher Modern Studies. Any feedback is always greatly appreciated. Contact us at modernityscotland@btconnect.com or join in the debates on the student forum on the modernityscotland site.

John McTaggart
October 2007

The Big Picture

These are historic days in Scottish politics. In 2007, the Scottish National Party (SNP) became the new Scottish Government. The SNP is committed to Scottish independence. Scotland's First Minister Alex Salmond pledges to deliver stable government, yet, at the same time, move the country towards separation from the UK.

His government has a parliamentary majority of just one MSP. Unlike the previous "Scottish Executive" (First Minister Alex Salmond changed the name to "Scottish Government" in August 2007) the SNP is governing without a coalition partner. Because of minority government, but also because of the Scottish Parliament's powerful committees and the greater time given to Private Bills, backbench MSPs have a much greater impact on decision making than MPs at Westminster.

It is important to distinguish between the Scottish Government and the Scottish Parliament. The Scottish Government is the devolved government for Scotland. It is responsible for most of the issues of day-to-day concern to the people of Scotland, including health, education, justice, rural affairs and transport. It manages an annual budget of more than £27 billion. "The Scottish Parliament" refers to all the MSPs, the parliament's rules, powers and structures.

The Scottish Parliament is now eight years old. We have had three elections to the Scottish Parliament. Voters are becoming better informed of the powers which are devolved and those which are reserved to Westminster. The Scottish Parliament has made many changes which have impacted on voters day to day lives. The Additional Member System of voting had, until the voting debacles of 2007, become more clearly understood by Scottish voters. The Scottish Parliament is settling in and becoming increasingly popular. There are even fewer criticisms over the cost of the parliament building, as the parliament becomes a major tourist attraction.

The Scottish Parliament's relationship with Westminster is likely to become increasingly interesting. Many voters in England are suspicious of the influence of "the Scots". Prime Minister Gordon Brown represents a Scottish constituency and has gone to great lengths to establish his "Britishness". We should expect grumblings about the West Lothian Question and finance to grow. The Conservatives, if elected at Westminster, would seek to bar Scottish MPs from voting on "English" issues.

Some MPs feel that, because of the Barnett formula, Scotland receives more of tax payers' money than it should. Relations between the two parliaments have been as smooth as they could be, but as we now have different parties in power in Holyrood and Westminster, more formal systems of communication perhaps need to be put in place.

In terms of local authorities, once again, we live in historic times. Labour, Scotland's leading party for fifty years, is no longer the dominant force in Scottish local authorities. It's now the SNP. The Single Transferable Vote (STV) has brought in numerous non Labour coalitions. The Council Tax could be on the way out. With nearly half of all councillors elected in 2007 taking office for the first time, a wind of change is taking place. Expect to see many more changes in Scottish local government.

Chapter 1: The Scottish Parliament and Scottish Government

Why a Scottish Parliament?

The last Scottish Parliament dissolved in 1707 with the Union of Crowns between Scotland and England.

Scotland however retained its own distinctive legal and education systems. Scottish interests were represented through parliamentary procedures in the House of Commons. The Cabinet post of Secretary of State for Scotland, with a Scottish Office staffed with Scottish civil servants, ensured that decisions affecting Scotland were addressed within the UK system of government.

Yet, famously, in 1999, the Scottish Parliament was reborn. It was temporarily housed in the General Assembly of the Church of Scotland in the Mound. But, in 2004, a stunning new parliament building at Holyrood in Edinburgh was built, at an eventual cost of £450 million. Why, after almost three hundred years, was there a need for a Scottish Parliament?

Many in Scotland desired a Parliament in 1979. However, a contentious referendum on devolution delivered a negative result. The years 1979 to 1997 saw economic and political differences between England, (particularly Southern England), and Scotland intensify. While Scotland's traditional, labour-intensive industries closed down, the City of London prospered. The 1980s was the decade when prosperity in England was matched with mass unemployment and poverty in central Scotland.

Politically, this economic divide was matched by a growing political divide. While the Conservative Party won three UK General Elections in a row, the Labour Party became increasingly popular in Scotland. Scottish voters resented being ruled by a Conservative Party they believed they had rejected in Scottish polling booths. Unpopular policies such as the "poll tax", introduced in Scotland a year ahead of its introduction in England, reinforced a mood that the "English" Conservatives were, at best, unaware of Scottish needs and, at worst, did not care.

There were occasional by-election triumphs for the pro-independence Scottish National Party, which was in the process of transforming itself from a fractious pressure group to a serious political force. A "Constitutional Convention", composed of a variety of political parties and civic groups, recommended the creation of a Scottish Parliament, to counteract the "democratic deficit" which it felt now existed.

When Tony Blair was elected Prime Minister in 1997, he pledged to "modernise" the UK constitution and create new political relationships. A referendum approved both the setting up of a Scottish Parliament and tax raising powers for the new parliament. Tony Blair's then Secretary of State for Scotland, Donald Dewar, set himself the task of preparing a "Scotland Bill" which would renew Scotland's place within the United Kingdom.

The Scottish Parliament would have certain powers "devolved" to it, while certain others powers would be "reserved by the UK Parliament at Westminster. A "Consultative Steering Group" (CSG) was set up to establish what it hoped would be a "new kind of politics". The CSG sought a modern parliament with values and procedures very different from the "old" politics of Westminster.

The devolution settlement, introduced by the 1997-2001 UK Labour Government, was an attempt to redefine relations between member nations within the whole of the United Kingdom, not just Scotland's relations with England. In Wales, a new National Assembly was created. In Northern Ireland, after years of conflict and bloodshed, a new devolved Assembly has been constructed too.

> **Activities**
>
> - What were the social/economic and political reasons behind the set-ting up of the Scottish Parliament?
> - What did Tony Blair hope to achieve by setting up devolved governments throughout the UK?

The Founding Principles of the Scottish Parliament

The CSG's four key principles for the Scottish Parliament are:

- # Accessibility
- # Accountability
- # Equal Opportunities
- # Sharing Power

Accessibility

The founders of the Scottish Parliament believed that Government at Westminster had become distant from the Scottish people. Not just geographically, but politically. Voter turnout rates were declining. Opinion polls showed that the public distrusted Members of Parliament and felt excluded from the political process. The Scottish Parliament therefore had to be accessible to the Scottish people.

All meetings of the Scottish Parliament in the Debating Chamber, and most committee meetings are open to the public. These can also be viewed live on the internet via the Scottish Parliament's webcast service www.holyrood.tv

Many of the Scottish Parliament's committee meetings have been held outside of Edinburgh to allow greater public access and participation. The

Public Petitions Committee, for example, has met in each of the eight electoral regions in Scotland. In 2006, the Environment and Rural Development Committee visited Stornoway, Oban and Inverness, as part of its scrutiny of the Crofting Reform Bill.

Petitions to the Parliament can be submitted online via the Parliament's website. In October 2006, school pupils from All Saints secondary school in Glasgow presented the 1000th petition to the Public Petitions Committee. The petition called on the Parliament to urge the Scottish Executive to investigate the impact on public health of cheaply available alcohol. A committee meeting was held at the school later that month.

From September 2006 to March 2007, the Scottish Parliament's Outreach Education service visited 269 classes, including further education colleges. The Scottish Parliament welcomes visitors seven days a week. There is a crèche facility for those wishing to take part in parliamentary business. The Scottish Parliament's Visitor Services team provides free tickets for committee meetings and parliamentary debates.

Since May 2004, over 8,000 young people have visited the Scottish Parliament, taking part in tours organised by the Scottish Parliament's Education department. The Scottish Parliament's Education service has organised many events for young people, including two Advanced Higher Modern Studies

seminars. The Scottish Parliament Information Centre (SPICe) provides an impartial research service, offering advice on issues such as freedom of information and data protection.

Accountability

Parliamentary procedures, such as First Minister's Question Time, hold the Scottish Government to account. First Minister's Question Time takes place every Thursday at midday. MSPs have the opportunity to ask oral questions directly to the First Minister and his ministerial colleagues. Written questions may be lodged at any time and MSPs will receive a written answer.

In 2001, First Minister Henry McLeish had to resign after a scandal over office expenses. It is widely believed that the "grilling" by Conservative leader David McLetchie at First Minister's Question Time led to his resignation. Ironically, David McLetchie himself was forced to resign as leader of the Scottish Conservatives in October 2005, when evidence of his alleged misuse of taxi expenses was unearthed by the media. This would not have been possible without the Scottish Parliament's Freedom of Information Act.

Equal Opportunities

The Scottish Parliament in its operation and its appointments recognises the need to promote equal opportunities for all. The Scottish Parliament seeks to "mainstream" equal opportunities in all aspects of its work.

While Westminster is notoriously un-family friendly in its working practices (debates sometimes go on until the early morning), the Scottish Parliament seeks to abolish any barriers which may prevent MSPs from playing their part in family life. The Scottish Parliament sticks to business hours of nine till five.

Parliamentary recesses are timed with Scottish school holidays. 33% of MSPs are female. Not perfect, but a much higher percentage than Westminster (19.2%). Scotland's figure is among the highest percentage of female representation in the world. In 2007, Bashir Ahmad of the SNP became Scotland's first ethnic minority MSP.

Sharing Power

The adoption of a proportional Additional Member System was designed to encourage a wider cross section of views to be held in the Parliament. Because of this, smaller parties such as the Greens and Scottish Socialists have, in the past, been able to have several MSPs elected.

> 33% of MSPs are female. Not perfect, but a much higher percentage than Westminster (19.2%)

Likewise, the Scottish Senior Citizens' Party has been successful in gaining representation.

Ordinary Scottish citizens can have an impact on policy. The Scottish Parliament's Public Petitions Committee considers any issues raised by members of the public which are brought to the Scottish Parliament in the form of a petition.

Committees in the Scottish Parliament

Unlike Westminster, the Scottish Parliament has no second chamber. Westminster has the House of Lords to play the role of "quality assuring" Government bills. In the absence of a revising chamber, the Scottish Parliament has a much more powerful committee system, which can propose, as well as scrutinise bills.

Activities

- Give examples of how the Scottish Parliament has been innovative in making Scottish politics accessible.
- What evidence is there that the Scottish Parliament can hold the Scottish Government to account?
- To what extent are there equal opportunities in the Scottish Parliament?
- To what extent has the Scottish Parliament shared power with the Scottish people?
- Overall, to what extent are the founding principles of the Scottish Parliament being met?

The Scottish Parliament committees are often referred to as "the engine room" of the Parliament. It is often said that this is where the real work of the Scottish Parliament takes place. MSPs who score points off each other in the debating chamber tend to play a more co-operative role alongside each other in committees. The committees have the statutory power to require anyone, including Scottish Government Ministers, to give evidence before them and to produce documents in connection with their inquiries

There are two types of Scottish Parliament Committee: Mandatory and Subject. Mandatory Committees deal with ongoing, long term matters. For example, the Finance Committee has a vital role to play in the passage of the Scottish Parliament's annual budget. The other mandatory committees include the Procedures, Standards, Audit, European and External Affairs, Equal Opportunities and Public Petitions Committees. The Scottish Parliament would always wish to be seen to audit such things as MSP expenses and parliamentary spending, hence the Mandatory Audit Committee.

By contrast, Subject Committees reflect the Ministerial demands of the current Scottish Government. Ministerial departments can change or be merged together. For example, the SNP Government elected in 2007 replaced the 2000-2007 Transport Committee with a "Transport, Infrastructure and Climate Change Committee".

This is more than a name change. It is an attempt to join up thinking between transport and the environment. With Green MSP Patrick Harvie

as Convener, one would expect this committee to produce frank and honest discussion. For example, the Green Party is likely to oppose the Scottish Government's plans to approve funds for a new Forth crossing.

In 2006-07 committees met 324 times, scrutinising 28 bills and 297 pieces of subordinate legislation. 1,460 outside witnesses gave evidence to Scottish Parliament committees. Video-conferencing has been used, enabling witnesses from locations such as Addis Ababa in Ethiopia to provide an input to decision making.

The Education Committee

In 2006-07, the Education Committee was chaired by Iain Smith MSP. Members of the Committee were Wendy Alexander (Lab), Rosemary Byrne (Solidarity), Lord James Douglas Hamilton (Con), Fiona Hyslop (SNP), Adam Ingram (SNP), Marilyn Livingstone (Lab), Kenneth McIntosh, Frank McAveety (Lab) and Dr Elaine Murray (Lab).

The Education Committee scrutinised legislation such as The Protection of Vulnerable Groups (Scotland) Bill and the Gaelic Language (Scotland) Act 2005. The Education Committee also reported on the implementation of the Teachers Agreement, taking evidence from teaching unions, head teachers representatives and other stakeholders such as Convention of Scottish Local Authorities (COSLA) and HM Inspectorate of Education.

Individual MSPs and organisations outwith the Scottish Parliament can have a direct impact on policy. Private Bills which have been considered by the Private Bills Committee include the construction of the Glasgow Airport Rail Link (GARL), the Edinburgh Airport Rail Link (EARL) and the Airdrie-Bathgate Railway Bill.

Activities

- Explain the difference between mandatory and subject committees.
- Why are the Scottish Parliament's committees described as "the engine room" of the parliament?
- In what ways has the Education Committee made a contribution to decision making in the Scottish Parliament?

The Effects of the Additional Member System (AMS)

The CSG supported an Additional Member System (AMS) for the Scottish Parliament because it believed a PR system would be less likely to produce majority government. The Labour Party tends to do well in traditional First Past the Post elections (FPTP). This is because FPTP rewards parties which have a strong, geographically concentrated support. Labour has strong support in working class communities. This tends to mean Labour MSPs get elected in these constituencies. The other parties' votes are more spread out across the country.

If the CSG had decided on a FPTP voting system, it is likely that Labour would have formed majority governments in the Scottish Parliament. Small wonder that Labour advocated such a voting system! The other parties in the CSG favoured a proportional system, such as the Single Transferable Vote (STV). STV delivers a very proportional result. The number of MSPs a party gets corresponds to the percentage of votes a party receives.

The Additional Member System makes it very difficult for any one party to have an overall majority of MSPs in the Scottish Parliament.

The CSG reached a compromise. The Scottish Parliament's AMS combines FPTP with proportional representation. Voters vote twice in Scottish Parliament elections. The first vote uses FPTP and elects a constituency MSP. The second vote is proportional and elects an additional seven "list" MSPs. There are 73 constituency MSPs and 56 list MSPs. To date, there have been three elections to the Scottish Parliament. Elections to the Scottish

Parliament, unlike Westminster, are at fixed dates, every four years. The next Scottish Parliament election will be in May 2011. The SNP won the 2007 Scottish Parliament election by the closest of margins. The SNP won 32.95% of the vote, Labour won 32.2 %.

Turnout in the election was 51.7% in the constituency vote and 52.4% in the regional vote. This is slightly up from 2003 where the turnout was 49.4% in both the constituency and regional vote. The turnout does not take into account the estimated 140,000 spoilt papers. Turnout varied on the constituency vote from 63.4% in Eastwood, East Renfrewshire to 33.4% in Glasgow Shettleston. Significantly, Eastwood is one of Scotland's wealthiest constituencies, Shettleston one of the poorest.

Some parties benefit more than others from the list element of the AMS. The SNP does well from the party list system, as do the Conservatives and, to a lesser extent, the Scottish Greens. Both of the Scottish Greens' MSPs have been elected from the second, "party list" vote. The Scottish Green Party has been particularly skilled at exploiting the AMS.

Robin Harper MSP, Lothians. Robin Harper became the Greens' first UK parliamentarian in 1999.

> **Arguably, the creation of the Scottish Parliament with its AMS, saved the Scottish Conservatives from political extinction.**

The Scottish Green Party only put up candidates in the second, list election. The Scottish Green Party knows how the FPTP system works. It knows its voters are spread out and are not concentrated in specific constituencies. The Scottish Green Party therefore knows it has little chance of winning any constituency MSPs.

Arguably, the creation of the Scottish Parliament with its AMS, saved the Scottish Conservatives from political extinction. It is one of the great ironies that the Conservatives originally opposed both the Scottish Parliament, and its voting system! In 1999, all 18 of the Conservatives MSPs were from the second, list vote. In 2007, the Conservatives managed to have four MSPs elected from constituencies, but the other thirteen are from the second, party list vote.

However, the AMS isn't always good for smaller parties. The Greens now have only two MSPs. The Scottish Socialist Party (SSP) and Solidarity Scotland lost all their MSPs at the 2007 Scottish elections. The electoral system can't be blamed for this though. It was the surge in support for the SNP which punished the smaller parties, not the voting system itself. The Scottish Socialist Party and Solidarity Scotland indulged in bitter in-fighting thus making the parties unattractive to voters.

Activities

- Why was the AMS introduced for elections to the Scottish Parliament?
- Which parties benefit from the AMS and why?
- Why might the AMS not always favour smaller parties?

Interview with Andy Kerr MSP, East Kilbride

Modernity: What do you think the Scottish Parliament has achieved?

Andy Kerr: In relative terms the Scottish Parliament remains a young parliament. However, I think its greatest achievement is bringing the governance of Scotland closer to the people directly affected by its decisions. The parliament is extremely accessible, MSPs are in their constituencies and in the parliament ready and willing to meet with individual constituents, voluntary organisations, community groups, businesses, trade unions and wider civic Scotland.

That in itself is an immense achievement as the parliament can therefore be close and responsive to the people it seeks to serve. It has also set up a number of new innovations which proved successful.

The Petitions Committee is a powerful committee of the Parliament, and ensures that everyone who brings a petition to the Scottish Parliament gets a proper response from it. This is not the case with all parliaments and how they deal with petitions.

In terms of access, the Parliament holds a number of Committees which are accessible to the public, and its evidence gathering sessions are wide and consultative. In terms of the innovations and the achievement of the Parliament in policy then I would argue that there are many.

The smoking ban has probably become the most famous innovation of the parliament but I would also cite mental health legislation, class sizes, nursery places, free central heating for pensioners, free bus travel for pensioners. In terms of the economy, the development of the bio-sciences and life-sciences industries and the employment record in terms of reducing unemployment, increasing employment, particularly among young people and many others which became too numerous to mention.

Modernity: Is the Scottish Government too powerful in its relations with the Scottish Parliament?

Andy Kerr: It would be an unwise government which would ignore the wishes of the parliament. This has been a guiding principle of government to date, and it is now down to Alex Salmond as First Minister to continue to respond to that agenda.

The Committees of the Parliament are extremely powerful and have their own ability to create legislation, therefore, any government which sought to ignore the will of Parliament could find itself dealing with legislation anyway. Particularly, as we now have a minority administration and the ability to ignore parliament is limited. Nonetheless, those decisions which do not require a legislative or statutory underpinning could be delivered by the government without any reference to parliament.

Modernity: To what extent has the Scottish Parliament created "consensus politics"?

Andy Kerr: I would view the delivery of consensus politics within the parliament as a myth. Whilst valuable work goes on in the committees on a cross-party and consensus basis, when it comes to political issues of the day, then the parliament divides down to traditional political boundaries.

Therefore, I would suggest that the parliament has not delivered to any great degree a consensual political environment.

Modernity: Are you in favour of the Scottish Parliament having new powers?

Andy Kerr: My first response to this question is what powers and why? As I find it surprising that, when you ask someone who is advocating more powers for the Parliament, they cannot describe to you which powers they want and what they would do with them. For instance, many advocate greater fiscal powers for the parliament and the ability to raise and reduce taxes both on business and individuals. However, they do not describe how they would use those powers if they had them.

The CBI advocate more powers for the parliament because they want to see taxation on business reduced, and others advocate powers for the parliament so that they can see taxes rise to increase investment in public services. Therefore, I believe the question is more appropriately put as: what powers would you like the parliament to have and what would you use those powers for?

However, in summary, I am of the view that, as our parliament develops, over the next few years there will be occasions whereby appropriate exchange of powers should be negotiated across the parliaments. This has already happened when the Scottish Government was given responsibility for the rail network in Scotland.

Modernity: Are you in favour of the AMS, or would you prefer a differing voting system?

Andy Kerr: I would prefer First Past the Post.

Modernity: What problems do you see a minority administration facing?

Andy Kerr: I believe that the current SNP minority administration is only facing the consequences of ill-conceived promises to the electorate which they knew fine well they could not deliver. What they are doing is using their minority status as an excuse for lack of delivery and if that was not a big enough excuse, they are now trying to blame Westminster for the lack of resources. Their ability to deliver rests with their ability to make tough decisions.

Modernity: In terms of the Scottish Parliament's relations with local government, do you think Scotland is over-governed?

Andy Kerr: In comparative terms throughout the world, Scotland is neither over-governed nor under-governed. Many other nations have more or less politicians.

My own view about this would be that we require to have Members of Parliament to address matters reserved to the UK Parliament/Government, we require to have MSPs to address devolved matters in the parliament and government, and lastly I do believe that there is a requirement to have local politicians in order to determine local policies in relation to many of the public services which we rely on every day.

Therefore, whilst the structures may change and move around and shifts may occur, I am not of the view that there is a need to take out a tier of Government.

> "Whilst valuable work goes on in the committees on a cross-party and consensus basis, when it comes to political issues of the day, then the parliament divides down to traditional political boundaries."

The Scottish Cabinet May 2007; L-R Kenny MacAskill Secretary for Justice, John Swinney, Secretary for Finance & Sustainable Growth, Nicola Sturgeon, Depute First Minister and Secretary for Health & Wellbeing, Alex Salmond, First Minister, Fiona Hyslop, Secretary for Education and Lifelong Learning, Richard Lochead, Secretary for Rural Affairs and the Environment.

Coalition and Minority Government

In 1999 and in 2003, the Scottish Labour Party won the Scottish Parliament election, but did not have a parliamentary majority over the other political parties. It decided to enter into a coalition with the 4th-placed party, the Scottish Liberal Democrats.

In 2007, the SNP won the Scottish Parliament election, but once again the winning party did not have an overall parliamentary majority. The SNP tried to secure a coalition with the Scottish Green Party and the Scottish Liberal Democrats. The Scottish Green Party agreed, but the Scottish Liberal Democrats refused to enter negotiations with the SNP unless the party dropped its flagship policy of a referendum on Scottish independence.

The SNP has decided to govern as a minority administration, something Scottish Labour chose not to do. Governing as a minority means that, in theory, legislation can be defeated by the combined forces of the opposition parties. Early in its term of office, the SNP was defeated on the issue of a proposed tram and airport rail network in Edinburgh. The SNP Government wished to scrap the network, saving £100 million for its other manifesto commitments.

The Labour/Liberal Democrat coalition avoided such parliamentary defeats by negotiating a "partnership agreement". Cabinet posts were divided on a pro rata basis. Scottish Labour, being the largest party, provided the First Ministers (there were three in the first six years of the Scottish Parliament), while Scottish Liberal Democrats Jim Wallace, and latterly Nicol Stephen, served as Depute First Minister.

In return for the safe passage of legislation, both parties compromised on policy. Scottish Labour agreed to introduce the Single Transferable Vote (STV) for local government elections. The Scottish Liberal Democrats agreed to fees, albeit deferred fees, for university tuition.

SNP Minority Government

Having been denied a coalition by the Liberal Democrats, the SNP had no choice but to govern as a minority. The SNP Government will have to win legislation, not by numerical strength, but by force of argument, on an "issue by issue basis".

This may not be as difficult as one would imagine.

In the first place, it is only *legislation* that has to be approved by the Scottish Parliament. The Scottish Government can govern for Scotland on many issues without the support of the parliament. Alex Salmond has referred to the Standing Orders of the Scottish Parliament, agreed by Labour's late First Minister

Donald Dewar. Outwith votes on legislation, these orders grant authority to the Scottish Government to ignore the will of the Scottish Parliament.

Depute First Minister Nicola Sturgeon did not need formal legislation to reprieve two Accident and Emergency wards. Likewise, Finance Minister John Swinney did not need legislation to freeze Council Tax increases for three years.

The contentious areas of the SNP's manifesto appear to have been kept back for later in the parliamentary term. Alex Salmond is keen to show the Scottish people that the SNP, and by implication Scottish independence itself, need not mean instability.

To this end, the First Minister established a non party political Council of Economic Advisers (CEA).

Depute First Minister Nicola Sturgeon did not need formal legislation to reprieve two Accident and Emergency wards.

The government will have great difficulty in having its flagship policy passed for a referendum on independence. But other items in the SNP's legislative programme are much less contentious. Opposition parties have little reason to oppose in principle the SNP's Rape and Sexual Offences Bill, which plans to make it easier to secure convictions in rape cases.

Likewise, there is a parliamentary consensus to support the Abolition of Bridge Tolls Bill, which will abolish tolls on the Forth and Tay Road Bridges. Similarly, it is beyond comprehension that opposition parties will unite to scupper the Glasgow Commonwealth Games Bill, proposed by the SNP.

True to form, First Minister Alex Salmond was shrewd in his choice of legislation. The eleven bills he chose for his first legislative programme were those for which it was easiest to gather all-party support. There will be lively debate and intense scrutiny in committee, possibly even significant amendment to his legislation. But, that is what the Scottish Parliament is there to do.

The CEA's membership includes two Nobel Laureates in economics. The CEA meets quarterly and advises the First Minister directly on ways to improve Scotland's economic growth rate.

This explains why an important election pledge like the abolition of the Council Tax, which is controversial, will be introduced later. A bill on a referendum for Scottish independence was changed into a wider, and more inclusive, "national conversation". Potential Scottish Parliament powers over broadcasting have been handed over to an all party/no party commission of the great and the good in the Scottish media.

However, it is in the Scottish Parliament's committees that a minority government may face its greatest challenge. The SNP is in a minority position on all of the Scottish Parliament's fourteen committees. The parliament's debating chamber is one battleground, and one where First Minister Alex Salmond excels.

But taking on majority opposition forces on another fourteen fronts may be a more difficult task. For example, the Local Government Committee is likely

First Minister Alex Salmond with his Council of Economic Advisers, Edinburgh, June 2007.

to examine proposals to replace the Council Tax with a Local Income Tax. One would expect a Labour Chair to apply a high level of scrutiny. Opposition parties can also use the committees to push forward committee bills.

Activities

- In 1999 and 2003, why did the winning Labour Party decide to enter into coalition government with the Liberal Democrats?
- In 2007, why has the winning SNP not entered into a coalition government?
- What difficulties will the SNP Government face in passing its legislation?
- In what ways has the SNP Government tried to overcome these difficulties?

Constituency and List MSPs

In the Additional Member System (AMS), the voter has two votes; one to vote for a constituency MSP, the other to vote for a regional list MSP.
The first vote is actually a traditional FPTP election.

For example, in Dunfermline East in the 2007 Scottish Parliament election, the Scottish Labour candidate, Helen Eadie, won more votes than her rivals and became the constituency MSP. However, under the AMS, Dunfermline East is part of the wider Mid Scotland and Fife constituency.

In order to give some compensation to the parties who may have secured a reasonable number of votes spread out across the wider constituency, list

seats (each of Scotland's eight regions have seven additional list members) are allocated according to the proportion of the vote each party receives.

In 2007, in the Scottish Parliament constituency of Dunfermline East, Helen Eadie was elected as the constituency MSP. There were also seven additional "list" MSPs elected, as part of the wider Mid Scotland and Fife region which includes Dunfermline East. So, for example, if a constituent in Dunfermline East has an issue in the area that requires the MSP's attention, he/she could go to Helen Eadie as the constituency MSP to do something about it. But, he/she could, in theory, approach a list MSP instead. The voter could, for example, consult Conservative MSP, Murdo Fraser, who is one of Mid Scotland and Fife's seven list MSPs.

This aspect of the AMS has been controversial. In August 2003, the then Labour MP Brian Wilson described list MSPs as "a waste of space". Labour tends to do better in traditional FPTP constituency elections and resents the fact that the AMS rewards "lesser" parties who may not have won what it sees as a "real" election. There can, therefore, be an element of rivalry between constituency and list MSPs. Constituency MSPs tend to see themselves as the

Helen Eadie MSP, Dunfermline East.

"real" MSP for the constituency. They, after all, won the constituency election.

It is perfectly possible to have a situation, as in East Kilbride, where Labour's Andy Kerr won the constituency seat of East Kilbride, in the process defeating SNP candidate Linda Fabiani.

Murdo Fraser, List MSP for Mid-Scotland and Fife

But, Linda Fabiani was elected as a list MSP as part of the wider Central Scotland constituency. Linda Fabiani has gone on to play a significant part in the SNP Government.

Constituency MSPs have claimed that they have to deal with bigger workloads than their list colleagues. They claim that list MSPs have more time to "cherry pick" issues and gain favourable local publicity. On the other hand, some list MSPs, such as Robin Harper, have a very high public profile and will attract a heavier workload than other, more low-key MSPs.

Robin Harper was the first Green representative to be elected to a UK parliament and is faced with many competing demands for his time. List MSPs play their full part in parliamentary debates and committees. They make themselves available to constituents across a wide geographical area. Perhaps it is difficult to generalise on which type of MSP performs the best job in a constituency.

Activities

- What is the difference between a "constituency" MSP and a "list" MSP?
- What factors may cause tensions between constituency and list MSP?
- Why is it difficult to generalise over the effectiveness of constituency or list MSPs?

Chapter 2: Devolution: The Settled Will of the Scottish People?

The late Labour leader John Smith described devolution as the "settled will" of the Scottish people. He believed that the creation of a Scottish Parliament would offer Scots the best of both worlds: control over the most immediate affairs, yet within the overall security of the UK.

This may yet be the case. Most voters in Scotland voted for pro-UK parties in the 2007 Scottish elections. But there are undoubtedly tensions. The arrival of the SNP in 2007 as the new Scottish Government, and the party's status as the largest party in Scottish local government, shows that there is a mood for change. It is likely that the SNP government will test the limits of Scottish decision making.

Powers of the Scottish Parliament

Even though there is now a Scottish Parliament, and the SNP is in charge of the Scottish Government, Scotland is NOT an independent country. Scotland is not a "sovereign" nation with control over its own borders and the protection of those borders. Scotland remains part of the United Kingdom of Scotland, England, Wales and Northern Ireland.

People entitled to live in Scotland are citizens of the United Kingdom. As evidence of this, when a new Scottish Parliament opens, the newly elected MSPs swear allegiance to the Queen. This has become the focus of protest by SNP MSPs. Like Westminster, all Bills passed by the Scottish Parliament have to receive the Royal Assent by the monarch before they can become law.

The Scotland Act makes it clear which powers have been reserved by UK Parliament in Westminster and the powers which have been devolved to the Scottish Parliament at Holyrood.

The Devolved Powers are those where the Scottish parliament has the power to make primary legislation.

Devolved Powers	Reserved Powers
Agriculture, Forestry and fishing	Abortion law
Education and training	Broadcasting
Environment	The Constitution
Health	Defence
Housing	Employment legislation
Law and home affairs	Foreign policy
Local government	Immigration
Natural and built heritage	Social Security
Planning	UK Fiscal Powers
Police and fire services	
Social work	
Sport and the arts	

Reserved Matters are issues where the power to make laws has been kept by the UK Parliament at Westminster in London.

Changes the Scottish Parliament has made

Since 1999, the Scottish Parliament has made a number of changes to social policy in Scotland. It is debateable whether these changes would have been made had there not been a Scottish Parliament.

Free personal care for the elderly

In 2002 the Scottish Executive took the decision to introduce free personal care for all elderly people in Scotland. This was a bold move and one which showed a "Scottish", rather than a British, approach to social policy. There have though been concerns that there is not equal access to free personal care across Scotland's 32 local authorities.

No tuition fees

Scottish students at Scottish universities do not pay their tuition fees. Nor are there are, unlike England, "top-up" fees to be paid on popular courses. However, the row over tuition fees will not go away. Controversially, the Scottish Executive, in July 2005, imposed a 42% increase in fees on English students who come to Scottish universities, provoking claims of discrimination. This decision was made in an attempt to reduce the number of so-called "fee refugees", English students who have headed to Scotland for their university education.

Free Bus scheme

Since 2005, elderly people in Scotland can now travel by bus anywhere in the country for free.

Ban on Smoking in Public Places

On March 26 2006, the Scottish Parliament ban on smoking in public places came into effect.

Activities

•   Why did the Scotland Act reserve powers such as defence, immigration and social security to Westminster?
•   To what extent is the Scottish Parliament financially independent?

17

Tensions in the devolved settlement

Why could it be said that because of the legislation passed by the Scottish Parliament, Scotland is becoming a different country from England?

The Labour Party in Scotland is a strong supporter of the devolution settlement, as agreed in the 1997 referendum. Those who support the existing powers of the Scottish Parliament, such as Labour and the Liberal Democrats, believe these powers strike the right balance between solving issues which need specific Scottish solutions and those which the UK, as a whole, is better able to deal with.

Secretary of State for Scotland, Des Browne MP, believes the 1997 devolution settlement is still valid.

Labour Scottish Secretary of State Des Browne has stated that "devolution was an event, not a process". Labour sees any extension of the Scottish Parliament's powers, especially with the SNP in government, as a "slippery slope" to separation from the UK.

The Scottish Conservatives opposed the creation of the Scottish Parliament, but the party is now committed to its success. The Scottish Conservatives remain firmly opposed to independence. So too do the Liberal Democrats. This is why the party declined the SNP's offer of coalition talks. The Scottish Greens are pro-independence. Despite the electoral calamity of losing five of the party's MSPs, partly because of the SNP Government's minority status, and also because both Robin Harper and Patrick Harvie are talented, the Greens' two remaining MSPs are likely to be very influential in this Parliament.

We are likely to see the First Minister Alex Salmond seek to extend the powers of the Scottish Parliament wherever possible.

First Minister Alex Salmond has suggested the creation of a Scottish Olympics team, instead of a British one. Alex Salmond has set up a "Broadcasting Commission" to examine whether broadcasting should become a devolved power. The First Minister has also changed the name of the Scottish Executive to "The Scottish Government"

There have also been a number of high profile issues which the Scottish Parliament has been unable to resolve, because these powers are reserved by Westminster. While immigration is clearly a UK issue, it has implications for Scotland. While decisions over asylum applications are for the Home Office of the UK Government to take, the children of asylum seeking families will often be housed in local authority accommodation and go to Scottish local authority schools. They are cared for by the social workers employed by Scottish local authorities.

These arrangements have been agreed between Scottish local authorities and the Home Office. In 2005, the case of the Vucaj family brought the issue of immigration to public attention. The Vucaj family were asylum seekers from Albania. They claimed that, because of the Balkans conflict in the early 1990s, their life was at risk if they returned to Albania. They wished to live in Scotland on a permanent basis. The family lived in Glasgow for five years, while their application for asylum was considered by the UK Home Office.

The Vucajs settled very well in Glasgow, and the three children were popular, successful pupils at Drumchapel High School. In 2005, the media reported that the family were taken from their home in Glasgow early in the morning by a deportation team from the UK Home Office. They were taken to England where they were then flown to Albania.

Supporters of the family alleged "inhumane" treatment of waking children and physically removing them from their home.

The issue clearly concerned First Minister Jack McConnell. It was not his decision to remove the family. The Scottish Parliament does not have this power. Immigration is a reserved power for Westminster. The Scottish Government cannot change the law over immigration any more than it can change the law on pensions or interest rates. But the Vucajs were a family living in Scotland and were looked after by Scottish local authorities.

It has been agreed that in future there will be a "protocol" between the UK Home Office and the Scottish Government over the removal of failed asylum seekers. In August 2006, Amal Azzudin, one of the Glasgow Girls was nominated for "Child of the Year" for her campaigning role for the Vucaj family. In October 2006, the Scottish Executive reached a compromise with the Home Office on immigration. The Vucaj case is a classic example of the complex interaction between policies reserved to Westminster (i.e. immigration and asylum) and those devolved to Holyrood. One would imagine that First Minister Alex Salmond will seek to establish greater powers for the Scottish Parliament over issues such as immigration.

The war in Iraq

There have been many angry exchanges in the Scottish Parliament over the war in Iraq. Defence, however, is a reserved power. The Scottish Government can discuss defence issues, as can MSPs in the Scottish Parliament. But, the Scottish Parliament has no authority over defence issues.

In July 2005, the Scottish Parliament's Standards Committee suspended four Scottish Socialist Party MSPs from the Scottish Parliament over their protests about the G8 summit being held at Gleneagles. They brandished placards during First Minister's Questions and then staged a sit-in protest. In 2006, opponents of the war in Iraq succeeded in pressurising the Scottish Parliament to reveal details of flights organised by the USA to transport terrorist suspects.

These so-called "rendition" flights had landed in Scotland. Civil rights protestors claimed that suspects were being denied human rights, and lobbied the Scottish Executive to stop supporting the USA in this matter. While First Minister Alex Salmond cannot make any decisions over British forces in Iraq, he can comment on the war in and out of Parliament. It is likely that he will!

Activities

- What initiatives has First Minister Alex Salmond embarked on to extend the powers of the Scottish Parliament?
- Why does the Vucaj case illustrate the complex relations between Holyrood and Westminster?
- To what extent are debates on issues such as Iraq, a waste of parliamentary time?
- To what extent is devolution the "settled will" of the Scottish people?

Funding the Scottish Parliament

In the financial year 2005/2006, the Scottish Parliament managed an annual budget of £27 billion. The Scottish Parliament's budget will rise to over £30 billion in 2007-2008. This money is passed to the Scottish Parliament in the form of a "block grant" from Westminster. The Scottish Parliament has the power to vary the basic rate of income tax (currently 20p in the pound) in Scotland by up to 3 pence in the pound.

The amount of money the Scottish Parliament receives in block grant from Westminster is decided by what is known as the "Barnett Formula", named after the Labour peer Joel Barnett. The Barnett formula is widely recognised as controversial. The perceived 'unfairness' of the Barnett Formula is often raised in association with the West Lothian Question. English MPs feel Scotland, in comparison to English regions, does too well from the Barnett formula.

Decisions by the Scottish Parliament to defer university tuition fees and introduce free personal care for the elderly have fuelled the arguments about how Scotland is financed. From a Scottish Nationalist viewpoint, the SNP claims that Scotland does worse from Barnett. It also feels that Scotland should not be given "pocket money" from Westminster's Scottish Secretary of State. The SNP would like the Scottish Parliament to have not just the ability to vary tax by 3p in the pound, but to have full "fiscal autonomy", which would mean the end of the block grant from

Westminster, and the Scottish Parliament would raise its own taxes. The Scottish Conservatives have been debating the concept of "fiscal autonomy" for Scotland. Fical autonomy has its attractions for the Scottish Conservatives who believe in the Scottish Parliament having the responsibility for its spending decisions.

But other Conservatives are concerned that fiscal autonomy will lead to "the slippery slope" to independence. The Scottish Liberal Democrats do not support fiscal autonomy, but, like the Scottish Conservatives, believe in cutting Scottish business rates to make investing in Scotland more attractive. The SNP support fiscal autonomy. This is for economic reasons. The SNP believes fiscal autonomy would allow Scotland to set tax rates which would attract global businesses.

The SNP greatly admires the "Celtic Tiger" economy of the Republic of Ireland. But, there is a political dimension to the fiscal autonomy debate too. If the block grant from Westminster was ended, Scotland would take one more step on the road to independence.

Alastair Carmichael MP

Lord Barnett feels it is time to end the Barnett formula. In 2004, he said, "It was never meant to last this long, but it has gone on and on and it has become increasingly unfair to the regions of England. I didn't create this formula to give Scotland an advantage over the rest of the country when it comes to public funding." The Liberal Democrats have called for reform to the Barnett Formula too.

Activities

- How does the Scottish Parliament raise its finances?
- Why do some English MPs criticise the Barnett formula?
- Why does the SNP criticise the Barnett formula?
- What alternatives are there to the Barnett formula?

The Challenge of Independence

Early in its term of office, The SNP Scottish Government published a White Paper on a proposed referendum on Scottish independence.

The ballot would ask voters whether they agree or disagree "that the Scottish Government should negotiate a settlement with the Government of a United Kingdom so that Scotland becomes an independent state". If passed by the Scottish Parliament, this referendum would take place some time before 2010, as promised in the SNP manifesto for the 2007 Scottish elections.

It is highly unlikely that the White Paper, as it stands, will be passed. The majority of MSPs are opposed to Scottish independence. Alex Salmond however was shrewd in his delivery of this key SNP manifesto promise. On constitutional issues, the SNP can only count on the votes of their 47 MSPs, plus presumably the two Green MSPs and the independent Margo MacDonald.

SNP activists, and presumably voters, would like independence, but they know most MSPs are against it. As are most MPs at Westminster. Constitutionally it is up to Westminster whether a Scottish Parliament gets any more powers at all, far less independence.

But, Alex Salmond has started a "national conversation" about independence. Members of the public have been asked to participate in a Scottish Government blog on whether independence, or other constitutional change such as greater powers over finance, is desirable. Thousands of people have commented.

"When even Lord Barnett is disowning the Barnett Formula, it is clear it has to go". Liberal Democrat Shadow Scottish Secretary, Alistair Carmichael MP.

The First Minister is playing a long game. He knows independence is not possible in this Scottish Parliament. Perhaps in the next one? An SNP First Minister could not possibly forget about Scottish independence. What point would there be in a SNP Scottish Government if he did? He must keep the possibility of independence on the agenda. Hence the "national conversation".

The First Minister will also try to extend the powers of the Scottish Parliament that little bit more, wherever he can, to gradually slacken the bonds of the UK. This explains the name change of the Scottish Executive and the creation of a Scottish Broadcasting Commission. Names are important. Alex Salmond will believe that if the Scottish people get used to terms such as "the Scottish Government", actually voting for a fully independent Scottish Government will not seem so daunting.

The SNP has led a long-running campaign for a separate, Scottish-produced, national and international news bulletin, commonly referred to as the "Scottish Six". Broadcasting however is a reserved power. The 2007 SNP manifesto has the commitment: "An SNP government will push for the devolution of broadcasting powers to the Scottish Parliament". Alex Salmond has set up a "Scottish Broadcasting Commission", chaired by Blair Jenkins, former head of news and current affairs at BBC Scotland.

Other eminent members of the commission are former Labour First Minister Henry McLeish and entertainer Elaine C Smith. Few people would like to see less Scottish programming on television. A non

party political commission examining all possibilities defuses accusations of the SNP "picking fights" with Westminster. The political capital will not be lost on Alex Salmond that, on the evening of Scotland's Euro 2008 victory over France, one of the national team's greatest ever results, BBC Scotland did not broadcast the Scotland game live, but England's home game against Russia.

Activities

- Why, despite the 2007 SNP election win, is Scottish independence unlikely in the short term?
- Explain the "long game" strategy of First Minister Alex Salmond.
- Why is the name change of the Scottish Executive psychologically important?
- Why did Alex Salmond decide to set up a non party political commission to examine whether broadcasting should be a devolved power?

A New Constitutional Settlement?

The Sunday Herald newspaper has launched a campaign to have a new Constitutional Settlement for Scotland. This would be along similar lines to the campaign, the Constitutional Convention, which designed the blue print for the Scottish parliament. The "Constitutional Commission" (CC), led by Canon Kenyon Wright, the driving force behind the setting up of the Scottish parliament, believes there are several reasons why the powers of the Scottish Parliament and its relationship with England should be re-examined.

Sovereignty of the People

The decision by Tony Blair to join the US in the war in Iraq, coupled with anti-terrorist legislation, has, according to the CC, eroded the "sovereignty" of the Scottish people.

First Minister Alex Salmond at Crystal Rig windfarm, Dunbar, June 2007.

Secondly, the fact that the constitutional debate dominated the 2007 Scottish election, and will in all likelihood dominate the next one too, means that some decision must be made about which powers the Scottish Parliament should have. Election campaigns are too party political to be the place to discuss these issues maturely. The CC believes that a non-partisan, all party convention could do the job better.

The rise of "Englishness"

It is argued that some kind of "English votes for English issues" system or the creation of an English parliament, is inevitable to solve the West Lothian question. It is better to plan ahead for this, than merely to react when it does happen.

Differing political values between England and Scotland

The CC believes that the growing differences of opinion on, for example, war in Iraq, tuition fees, care for the elderly, immigration and the wealth gap mean that a political solution needs to be reached to accommodate Scotland and England's diverging political cultures.

Activities

Sum up the main arguments for re-visiting Scotland's constitutional settlement with the UK.

The Role of the First Minister

There have been four First Ministers, in total, since 1999. Donald Dewar died. Henry McLeish had to resign after a financial scandal. Jack McConnell became First Minister in November 2001.

Alex Salmond replaced Jack McConnell as First Minister in May 2007 after the SNP won, by a margin of one, the most MSPs in the Scottish Parliament. He was elected by all MSPs, as all First Ministers are. This stands in contrast to Westminster, where only the dominant party selects the leader.

The First Minister has the role of chairing the Scottish Cabinet, which meets on Wednesday mornings. Like the UK Cabinet, the Scottish Government operates on the basis of collective responsibility. This means that all decisions reached by Ministers, individually or collectively, are binding on all members of the Government. Ministers must publicly support collective Cabinet decisions.

Like the UK Prime Minister, the First Minister has the power of "hire and fire" over his Cabinet. Unlike Jack McConnell, Alex Salmond has no coalition partner to appease in his selection of government Ministers. Alex Salmond's Cabinet team is composed solely of SNP MSPs. Alex Salmond has trimmed the

Scottish Government down from nine departments to six, thus meaning a smaller team of Ministers. There are six Cabinet Secretaries, including the First Minister.

Unlike the Prime Minister, the First Minister cannot choose the date of the next election. Scottish Parliamentary elections are at fixed times, every four years. His main role as First Minister is to represent Scotland in the areas that are reserved to the Scottish Parliament. The First Minister is expected to have a vision for the country and to lead the country in a positive direction. His campaigns will cut across and permeate the work of all government departments.

Alex Salmond's first 100 days

On May 23 2007, Alex Salmond set out, in almost Presidential fashion, the priorities of his "first 100 days":

- The appointment of a Council of Economic Advisers to provide independent advice on making the most of opportunities in the global economy
- Scotland to be nuclear free and to take the lead in the 'green energy revolution' and the development of renewable technology
- The abolition of tolls on the Forth and Tay road bridges

The departure of the previous Labour/Liberal Democrat coalition does not mean that all the previous Scottish Executive's plans will be replaced. Many of these initiatives had won cross party support. For example, previous First Minister Jack McConnell set himself the task of making Scotland a more tolerant, outward-looking country. To this end, he led campaigns such as the "One Scotland" campaign, which seeks to combat racism and sectarianism.

In his acceptance speech as First Minister, Alex Salmond paid tribute to the work done by Jack McConnell in these areas. Likewise, Jack McConnell's pro enterprise agenda is likely to be taken forward by Alex Salmond's Cabinet. Initiatives such as the Curriculum for Excellence in Scotland's schools may be given a different focus. But the overall strategy will be the same: to improve the skills of Scotland's young people by promoting more creative, life-long approaches to learning. First Minister Alex Salmond is even less likely than Jack McConnell to take a back seat in international affairs. While he has no power over reserved issues, it is unlikely First Minister Alex Salmond will pass up the opportunity to express an opinion.

The First Minister is accountable for the actions of himself and the Scottish Government at First Minister's Question Time. This weekly slot is essentially political theatre rather than a forum for decision making. It is often good entertainment value, as rival politicians attempt to score points and embarrass the First Minister and the Government.

Jack McConnell has been succeeded by Wendy Alexander as Opposition leader in the Scottish Parliament. Her primary job is to hold the First Minister to account. She will use First Minister's Questions to put the media spotlight on any weaknesses shown by Alex Salmond. Unlike previous Opposition leaders, her chances of inflicting defeat on the Scottish Government are good. The SNP does not have an overall majority in the Scottish Parliament. In fact, it is very much in an overall minority position.

Alex Salmond's Scottish Government has 47 MSPs who face a potentially combined opposition of 81 MSPs. (Presiding Officer, the Conservatives' Alex Fergusson will not vote, except in a tied vote). Jack McConnell's Labour/Liberal Democrat coalition was able to push through legislation against the wishes of opposition MSPs. By contrast, the SNP minority government will rely on Parliamentary support for its legislation on an issue by issue basis.

However, Wendy Alexander has to decide the severity of the opposition the SNP will face. Should Labour oppose SNP legislation simply because it is SNP legislation, Labour may come across to the public as petty and small-minded.

Relations with Westminster

Differences are likely to arise in the Scottish Government's relationship with Westminster. Labour was the dominant party in the old Scottish Executive. Labour was in power at Westminster. There was a consensus on the devolution settlement. The two parliaments worked in partnership. Now, we have two different parties in the relationship, one of whom is seeking a divorce! The reason for the existence of the SNP after all is to sever Scotland's ties with Westminster and establish Scotland as an independent, sovereign country.

Jack McConnell, as First Minister, was very careful not to speak for Scotland on defence issues, which are reserved to Westminster. He was also reluctant to get involved in debates in the Scottish Parliament about the war in Iraq, as he had no authority over these issues. A minority First Minister is a new concept in Scottish politics, and we shall have to wait and see the impact of minority status on the powers of the First Minister. As First Minister, Jack McConnell, arguably, pushed the boundaries of his duties and responsibilities. Under his leadership, the Scottish Executive moved into the international arena, which, it could be said, is the role of the Westminster-based UK Foreign Secretary.

Scotland has entered partnerships to bring Chinese students to Scotland and to assist poverty stricken Malawi. Alex Salmond is likely to assert the First Minister's powers in relation to external Scottish affairs. To what extent Westminster, in the form of Prime Minister Gordon Brown, attempts to rein in the First Minister remains to be seen.

Activities

- What is meant by Cabinet "collective responsibility"?
- Describe the roles of the First Minister.
- Why has it been claimed that Alex Salmond has adopted a "Presidential" style of leadership?
- In what ways did First Minister Jack McConnell push the boundaries of the First Minister's responsibilities?
- Why might one reasonably expect First Minister Alex Salmond to push these boundaries further?

Scottish Representation at Westminster

Who speaks for Scotland? Is it the First Minister of the Scottish Parliament? Or is it Westminster's Secretary of State for Scotland? Prior to devolution, the Secretary of State for Scotland was the uncontested voice of the nation. The Secretary of State for Scotland is in charge of the Scotland Office. He has a seat in Cabinet. But, now we have a First Minister, one would assume he is the first minister!

Secretary of State for Scotland

Constitutionally, the Secretary of State for Scotland represents Scotland at a UK level in Cabinet. Since the creation of the Scottish Parliament however, there has been confusion and debate as to the value of the post. This intensified in June 2003, when Tony Blair replaced Helen Liddell as Secretary of State with Alastair Darling, then abolished the post, then brought it back again, but combined it with UK Transport!

The fact that the post is no longer officially "Secretary of State", but is combined with another brief, is evidence that it is no longer as vital or prestigious as it used to be. The fact remains though that the Secretary of State speaks on behalf of Scotland on reserved matters, such as defence.

The Secretary of State also has the role of liaising between Westminster and the Scottish Government, on matters such as the Barnett Formula which decides the level of block grant the Scottish Parliament receives.

The Secretary of State for Scotland is responsible for the conduct of Parliamentary elections in Scotland, a

First Minister Alex Salmond representing Scotland at the UEFA Cup Final, Hampden Park, Glasgow, May 2007.

power which has come under close scrutiny since the debacle of the 2007 Scottish elections.

Now there are two very different parties in power, the post of Secretary of State for Scotland has become a very political one. Alex Salmond has demanded that Westminster return £23 million of "stolen" funds for free personal care for the elderly. Alex Salmond will resist Labour's plans to renew nuclear power in Scotland. Alex Salmond has set in motion a "national conversation" over Scottish Independence and published a white paper on the country's constitutional future.

Under the terms of the Scotland Act 1998, Scottish representation at Westminster has been reduced from 72 seats to 59. These 59 MPs, overwhelmingly Labour, perform their traditional role as Members of Parliament representing constituents. They can debate and vote on all reserved issues, such as defence and the budget, but also on issues which affect only those living in England, such as university tuition fees. Prime Minister Gordon Brown represents the Scottish constituency of Kirkcaldy and Cowdenbeath.

MPs from Scotland can also participate in Scottish Questions and sit on the House of Commons' Scottish Affairs Committee. In what has become known as "the West Lothian Question", many English MPs, particularly Conservative MPs, have challenged the status of Scottish representation at Westminster.

The West Lothian Question

There are two aspects to the West Lothian Question: firstly, how can it be right that MPs elected to Westminster from Scottish constituencies have no ability to affect the issues of their constituents on matters which have been devolved to the Scottish Parliament?

Secondly, power over certain Scottish affairs has been devolved to the Scottish Parliament; MPs representing Scottish constituencies in the Parliament of the United Kingdom have the power to vote on issues, such as education, which affect England but English MPs do not have the power to vote on devolved Scottish issues. How can this be right?

The West Lothian question was first posed by Labour MP Tam Dalyell in the 1970s. He warned that the creation of a Scottish Parliament would create a serious constitutional difficulty. Tony Blair's Labour Government has relied on votes from Scottish MPs to pass contentious legislation which applies only in England. These included two votes on Foundation hospitals and two on university tuition fees.

One fringe party, the English Democrats, has called for an English Parliament to be created. English opposition to Gordon Brown's premiership is not based on his nationality, but on his political status. Constitutionally, Gordon Brown is the MP for a Scottish constituency, Kirkcaldy and Cowdenbeath.

The Liberal Democrats believe in a federal solution to the UK's constitution. They would like to see devolution, not just for Scotland, Wales and Northern Ireland, but for regions in England too. They believe this would end calls for an "English Parliament" and Scottish independence as each region would be able to address the specific needs of its area, all within the wider UK.

If the Conservatives were to win the next General Election Conservative leader David Cameron would block Scottish MPs from voting on legislation that applies only to England. Cameron's solution has been drawn up by former Scottish Secretary of State, Sir Malcolm Rifkind. It is being called the "East Lothian answer," as Sir Malcolm lives in East Lothian.

The East Lothian answer would not involve a separate English Parliament, which critics fear could lead to the break-up of the UK. Instead, there would be a "grand committee," composed only of MPs representing English constituencies. This committee would be convened at Westminster whenever Parliament is considering legislation deemed by the Speaker of the Commons to apply only to English constituencies. The revival of the Northern Ireland assembly means that Northern Ireland MPs would also be excluded from the committee. So would Welsh MPs if, as expected, Wales gets a more powerful law-making body which is able to pass primary legislation.

> "The West Lothian Question is the unfinished business of devolution."
>
> Sir Malcolm Rifkind MP

Sewel motions

Lord Sewel's ruling in the Scotland Act declares that "there will be instances where it would be convenient for legislation on devolved matters to be passed by the UK parliament".

To date, Sewel motions have been used on over 60 occasions, covering issues such as gambling, tobacco advertising and rights of gay couples. On these occasions the Labour/Liberal Democrat Scottish Executive either passed the issue to Westminster to apply a ruling or accepted a law passed at Westminster to apply in Scotland.

An example of this was the decision by the 1999-2003 Scottish Executive to use a Sewel motion to allow Westminster to legislate on the rights of gay couples. This was a potentially controversial issue. The Scottish Executive had faced strong opposition to its decision to repeal Section 2A of the Local Government Act which banned the discussion of homosexuality in schools.

The SNP have claimed that Sewel motions undermine the powers of the Scottish Parliament. Labour on the other hand sees Sewel motions, in certain circumstances, as sensible and appropriate, whenever a UK wide ruling is required. It will be interesting to see if First Minister Alex Salmond uses any Sewel motions!

Activities

- What are the roles of the Secretary of State for Scotland?
- Why might some people claim that the post of Secretary of State for Scotland is no longer so important?
- What opportunities do MPs representing Scottish constituencies have to influence legislation in the House of Commons?
- Why is there some resentment among MPs from English constituencies over the West Lothian Question?
- What solutions have been offered to solve the West Lothian Question?
- Why have Sewel motions been controversial?
- To what extent is devolution the "settled will" of the Scottish people?

Chapter 3: Local Government in the Devolution Era

Local Government is Scotland's biggest employer, bigger than the National Health Service. In 2005-06, total expenditure by Scottish local government was £18.4bn. In 2006, there were 230,300 full-time employees in local government (excluding police, fire and related services). Of this total, 57,700 (25%) were teachers, 35,900 (16%) other education staff, 44,600 (19%) social work staff and 92,000 (40%) other staff.

The Roles of Local Government

The roles of Scotland's local authorities were set out in the 2003 Local Government in Scotland Act.

Providing Services

Local authorities have responsibility for the planning, resourcing and direct provision of a wide range of services. These include education, housing, social work, economic development, public protection, planning, leisure and recreation. It is hard to think of being able to go through a typical day without coming into contact with a service delivered bt a local authority.

Additional methods of service provision have developed in recent years. These include working in partnership with other public agencies and commissioning services from the voluntary and private sectors, for example, community planning partnerships and local economic forums.

Strategic Planning

Local authorities provide a long-term strategic planning framework setting long term objectives for their area. This framework directs both the policies and activities of internal functions and seeks to influence the priorities of external organisations within their areas.

Regulation

Local authorities also have regulatory functions, such as the granting of certain licences (e.g. taxi drivers and public houses), and registration and inspection functions (e.g. environmental health).

Community Leadership

This is a relatively new role for local authorities which involves addressing issues which do not fit neatly within the responsibility of any single agency. Such cross-cutting issues include promoting social inclusion, ensuring community safety and dealing with environmental concerns.

The Glasgow 2014 Commonwealth Games is a classic example of the role of local government in Community Leadership.

The Local Government in Scotland Act 2003 designated local government as the key agency in the community planning process in providing local authorities with a 'power of well-being'.

Glasgow City Council's successful bid for the 2014 Commonwealth Games is a classic example of a local authority promoting "well being". The 2014 Commonwealth Games will have a major impact on the wider Scottish economy and sectors such as tourism and hospitality. Glasgow Chamber of Commerce estimates that around £300m could be invested in Glasgow. The east end of the city has suffered from long term unemployment for many years. Now, there will be around 1,000 new houses built. The athletes village, a new indoor athletics facility and a velodrome will also be built in the east end. Just important, community spirit can be built, up to 2014 and beyond.

Local authorities continue to play their long standing role in providing political leadership at a local level. In Scotland, it is elected representatives, accountable to local people, who make multi million pound decisions over vital services such as housing and education.

The 2007 Scottish local authority elections transformed the dynamic of local representation. The Scottish public no longer has just one local councillor for their area. The Single Transferable Vote (STV) has created multi member constituencies with voters having three or four councillors available for consultation.

STV has strengthened local democracy in the sense that there are no longer "safe seats" for sitting councillors. If a councillor does not represent local constituents effectively, the voter can vote for an alternative candidate within the same party or vote for an alternative party.

Relations between Scottish Parliament and Local Government

Scotland's 32 local authorities are passionate advocates of their own distinct identity. They believe services, such as education, are best delivered locally, administered by professionals who are appointed by elected local representatives. However, local government is a devolved power. Many of the other powers the Scottish Parliament has had devolved to it, such as education and housing, are services traditionally provided by local government. Tensions undoubtedly exist.

The current "Minister for Finance & Sustainable Growth" is John Swinney. Local Government is part of the Minister's remit. The previous local government Scottish Executive Minister, Labour's Tom McCabe, had the title of "Minister for Finance and Public Service Reform".

John Swinney MSP, North Tayside, Minister for Finance & Sustainable Growth.

What's in a name? The previous Labour/Liberal Democrat coalition clearly had the reform of public services on its mind. Some claim that Scotland is now "over governed". Scotland, it is claimed, is a small nation and why should we have 32 different solutions to issues of criminal justice, or education, to name but two?

Activities

- Give examples of local authorities, especially your own local authority, fulfilling their roles in the governance of Scotland.
- Why has the introduction of STV changed the relationship between councillor and voter?

Criminal Justice

The 2003-2007 Scottish Executive, as part of its so-called "war on neds", championed the use of Anti-Social Behaviour Orders (ASBOs) to tackle bad behaviour across the country. The power to impose an ASBO comes from the Scottish Government. It is local authorities who implement ASBOs (or not as the case may be).

"We have always supported the line the Executive has taken on this. It's not political pressure that's driving what we are doing, it's pressure from Edinburgh residents. The streets belong to hard-working people who live here, not the yobs who make people's lives a misery."

Donald Anderson, former Labour leader of City of Edinburgh Council.

Not all local authorities implemented ASBOs as enthusiastically as First Minister Jack McConnell would have liked.

In 2006, the highest ASBO rates occurred in local authorities such as Edinburgh, West Lothian, Borders and North Ayrshire This does not mean that there is necessarily more anti-social behaviour in these areas, just that these local authorities were more robust in their enforcement of ASBOs.

By contrast, Glasgow City Council did not obtain a single ASBO between April 2003 and March 2006. Glasgow City Council's reluctance to use ASBOs can be compared with City of Edinburgh Council, where 71 ASBOs were served in the same period, 41 in 2005-6 alone.

In 2005/06 there were 11,555 recorded crimes of vandalism, reckless damage and malicious mischief within City of Edinburgh boundaries alone, a figure that was up 47% from the previous year. Across Scotland, nearly 330 such incidents a day were recorded in 2005-06.

Education

Education in Scotland is one of local authorities' most treasured services. Each local authority is very different in its approach to education, in spending and in its priorities. Yet, there are increasing national Scottish Government initiatives that may cut across local authority priorities.

The 2003-2007 Scottish Executive decision to lower class sizes in English and Maths is one. So too was the decision to recruit an extra 53,000 teachers. Why 53,000 teachers? Where did this figure come from? Which local authorities will the teachers go to? In any case, do all local authorities need extra teachers? Do local authorities have the funds to pay the salaries of 53,000 teachers? In which subjects will these teachers be recruited? If these centrally made decisions are to be successfully delivered, they require the expertise of local authorities on the ground.

But, there is scope for peaceful co-existence. The Scottish Government makes policies for the whole country while each of Scotland's local authorities has their own specific needs. Co-operation between the Convention of Scottish Local Authorities (COSLA), which represents local authorities, and the Scottish Government is ongoing. It rarely makes news, but there are regular meetings and contact to decide how Scottish Government policies can most effectively be implemented.

John Swinney is expected to reach an agreement with COSLA which will freeze Council Tax increases across all 32 local authorities. In return, the Scottish Government is likely to grant local authorities greater control over the funding of local services. Whether this enables the SNP to fulfill its 2007 Scottish Parliament election commitment to reduce class sizes remains to be seen. Local authorities, not all governed by the SNP, are likely to have a much bigger say.

Activities

- Why might there be tension between the Scottish Parliament and local government?
- Why do some people claim that Scotland is over governed?
- Why can it be difficult for the Scottish Government to implement a social policy uniformly across the whole country?

Interview with Rory Mair, Chief Executive of COSLA

Modernity: What is COSLA's role?

Rory Mair: COSLA represents Scottish local government to its external partners e.g. Westminster, Holyrood and other big players such as Scottish Enterprise or Scottish National Heritage.

Instead of these organisations negotiating with 32 different councils, we can commit our members to acting in a certain way.

We are part and parcel of any decision making process where local government plays a part. If you think of young people, we provide housing, schools, buses to schools, leisure facilities, parks, care for young people who get into difficulties. We are a big part of the day to day life of Scotland!

Take, for example, the ban on smoking in enclosed public spaces. This Act was passed in the Scottish Parliament. But it would have been unworkable without our input in providing environmental services in health or in litter. We would have had a law but not a mechanism.

Modernity: Given that you have 32 members and given that we now have local authorities of a whole variety of political complexions, how does COSLA know what your members' views are?

Rory Mair: We have an extensive political engagement process. I would last about 3 minutes as Chief Executive of COSLA if I just represented the views of Rory Mair!

COSLA has six executive groups, each with a chairperson or spokesperson.

We have leaders meetings of the 32 local government leaders once per month.

We also have Convention meetings which are made up of a wider group of delegates, based on the political complexion of each local authority, who meet several times a year.

The 2007 elections have made many changes to the political leadership of local authorities. I would anticipate that in future we may have more Convention meetings, to take into account the more varied political leadership which now exists across and within local authorities.

However, it's not just about reacting to political decisions taken elsewhere. It is important to get ahead of the game by reading party manifestos, anticipating likely policy decisions and asking what can we do, how can we help make better policy?

Modernity: How does the decision making process between COSLA and the Scottish Government work?

Rory Mair: It is inconceivable that any administration would consider changes to major public services, e.g. education, without consulting COSLA. Education in Highland Council, for example, is very different from education in Glasgow. Highland Council is larger than Belgium! We have specialist knowledge and representation from all the different communities across Scotland. We believe it is important that what happens in schools reflects the community schools are part of.

We have meetings with Scottish Government ministers around 4-5 times per week.

There are two different kinds of relationship we have with the Scottish Government. The first kind is what you could call transactional. For example, how can we help you deliver your policies more effectively? The second is where we take up the role of lobbying the Scottish Government for something we want. For example, the previous Scottish Executive was considering an American style "Correctional Agency" to fast track offenders into the criminal justice system. We felt this would have undermined the

Rory Mair, Chief Executive of COSLA

good work our social work professionals do and explained this to the Executive. We managed to dissuade them from pursuing this policy.

Modernity: Since devolution, the Scottish Parliament now has over arching powers over local government. Do you feel we are over governed?

Rory Mair: Central Government has always had over arching powers over local government. The difference now is that central government is along the road, rather than being in London and that is better for decision making.

It is still all quite new, but there is a growing understanding that the Scottish Parliament should set national priorities and allow local government room to work within these national priorities.

We are not just a delivery agent, we have a central part to play in the decision making process.

Scotland is not over governed. Scandinavian countries, countries we admire for all sorts of reasons, have many more politicians than we have. There are other countries, Italy for example, where local government's role is written into the constitution.

Other countries have local governments who have much more financial independence, We only have the power to raise around 20% of our finance

through Council Tax. 80% comes from central government.

Modernity: But are there not too many councils all doing the same thing? Could economies of scale not be made by merging smaller authorities together?

Rory Mair: At the moment, local councils come together to deliver some services. The three Ayrshires for example (East Ayrshire, North Ayrshire and South Ayrshire Councils) come together for single service delivery, but have slightly different local service, depending on the needs of local communities.

There are other possibilities. The 32 local authorities all employ lawyers. Why not have a common pool of lawyers we could all use?

Modernity: What do you see as COSLA's biggest achievement?

Rory Mair: I think it's getting to where we are now in establishing local government as a fundamental part of the governance of Scotland; central government acknowledging that local councils can provide a service that is distinctive and that is governed by people who were elected.

The idea of the "common good" is still prevalent in Scotland and Alex Salmond has spoken of this. There is still some notion that people are part of a wider community. In England there is more of an attitude where people may say "I want my bin emptied, I don't care if it's emptied by a company from France, I just want it emptied". In Scotland, we may accept that education may be a higher priority at times than other services and that is for the common good, whether I personally benefit from it right here, right now.

> "I would last about 3 minutes as Chief Executive of COSLA if I just represented the views of Rory Mair!"

STV and Local Government

The Single Transferable Vote (STV) was introduced to Scottish local elections for the first time in 2007. STV was introduced as part of the Partnership Agreement of the 2003-2007 Labour/Liberal Democrat Scottish Executive. The 2000 Kerley Report into participation in local government led to calls from the Scottish Liberal Democrats to reform the status of local councillors.

> "Democracy, by its very definition, is a matter that involves the whole population. We are concerned that a significant proportion of the population appears to take little part in the democratic process".
> Richard Kerley

Kerley was concerned at the low turnout for local government elections. Turnouts for local government by-elections had gone as low as 12% in some council wards.

Kerley recommended that a STV voting system be introduced. The traditional FPTP system provided the Labour Party with a massive advantage. Scottish Labour controlled the bulk of Scotland's 32 local authorities, often with a minority of the overall vote. Many elections were "safe" Labour seats and the results a foregone conclusion. Kerley felt that safe Labour seats created a lack of competition at election time, which possibly led to less effective government.

A new STV voting system would lead to a wider group of political parties having a realistic prospect of winning seats at council elections. It may result in a "new broom" of local councillor being elected. Kerley recommended that the old system, of part-time councillors being paid expenses only, be replaced with full time councillors being paid a salary instead.

These recommendations were implemented by the Labour/Liberal Democrat Scottish Executive. Existing councillors were offered redundancy payments. A new voting system was put in place. New voting wards were created. These wards would be larger and, as part of the STV system, would have more than one local councillor representing the voters.

The first STV Scottish local government election took place on May 3 2007. The results were dramatic. The political landscape of Scottish local government was transformed, perhaps permanently.

2007 Scottish local government elections

It took some time before all of Scotland's 32 local authorities were able to put a governing administration in place. FPTP tended to produce majority one-party control. STV brought in many coalition administrations. Only six local authorities had single party 'minority' administrations: Clackmannanshire (Labour), East Ayrshire (SNP), Inverclyde (Labour), Midlothian (Labour), North Ayrshire (Labour) and, South Ayrshire (Conservative). The remaining 21 local authorities had multi-party coalitions forming a governing administration.

The SNP replaced Labour as the largest party in Scottish local government. In local authorities such as City of Edinburgh and West Lothian, coalitions were formed in order to exclude Labour. It seemed that, after years of Labour rule, other parties were ganging up against Labour. On the other hand, in East Dunbartonshire, Labour and the Conservatives formed a coalition to keep the SNP out!

STV has provided an entirely new style of politics. Parties which used to be sworn enemies of each other now need to find common ground. Parties, chiefly Labour, who used to take ruling alone for granted, now have to work with other parties. Even in Glasgow, which remains Labour-controlled, Labour has a strong SNP opposition, with some Green Party councillors in existence too.

There is also a new broom. Many "old" councillors accepted the redundancy packages that were offered by the Scottish Executive. 48% of councillors elected in 2007 were elected for the first time. The days of local councils being dominated by middle-aged men appear to be over. Aberdeen City Council has several youthful SNP councillors: Callum McCaig was just 22 years old when elected; Education spokesperson, Councillor Kirsty West was just 21 when elected; her younger brother John, at the age of 18, became Aberdeen's Deputy Lord Provost. He has been responsible for chairing full council meetings, at which multi million pound decisions have been made.

Activities

- What was the main concern of the Kerley report?
- Why might the traditional FPTP voting system have led to low turnouts in local authority elections?
- Why did the Scottish Labour Party agree to the introduction of STV even though it knew it may lose elected councillors?
- In what ways has STV changed the political landscape?

Financing Local Government

The 2003 Local Government Act placed a duty on local authorities to secure "best value". It also put community planning on a statutory basis and provided local authorities with a power 'to advance well-being'.

What is "Best Value"?

The concept of Best Value was first introduced in the 1990s by previous Conservative Governments, which also brought in Compulsory Competitive Tendering (CCT) to local government services, for example in the provision of school meals.

The Conservatives challenged the acceptance that local authorities could provide, for example, school meals. In theory, McDonalds or some other private provider might provide better value in quality and cost; why should McDonalds not have the opportunity to challenge the local authorities' provision of school meals?

School meals therefore, like all other local authority services, are the result of a best value process. Providers, including "in house" providers, are required to bid for the opportunity to provide a

service. The bid will be scrutinised by the local authority. Any competing bids will be scrutinised too. The successful bid will be the one which offers "best value" to you, the consumer of the service.

Best Value is a continuous drive to improve quality, effectiveness and efficiency of the Council's services. Using the criteria of the 4 "Cs", local authorities:

- Challenge how and why they provide the service
- Compare the cost and quality of the service
- Compete to see if value for money is provided
- Consult users of services on their views.

Local authorities have moved towards involving communities in decision making (consultation, questionnaires, Citizens Panels, Business Panels) and also reporting on their performance by publishing statistics via newsletters and websites.

Education is a good example. Over 90% of school pupils in Scotland go to schools provided by a local authority. In order to show that schools are providing best value to pupils, parents and the local community, there are school inspections by HM Inspectorate of Education (HMIe).

HMIe, on behalf of the Scottish Government, prepare "Quality Indicators", against which school managements evaluate their performance. Schools are regularly inspected and the results published in local papers and the HMIe website. Schools, by law, must show that they are continually seeking to improve the quality of education they offer.

Local authorities now have recycling targets which they are legally responsible to meet. Many local authorities have moved to fortnightly litter collections. Households are being encouraged to recycle plastic, paper and garden rubbish. Roads have a big impact on the environment too. There is evidence of bus lanes and cycle lanes provided by local authority to help improve the environment.

Some, of course, question the value of these initiatives. Are they of best value to bus users, car drivers, and how do we truly know the environmental value? Bus lanes can lie empty. Sometimes there are one or two people on buses (and no cyclists), while car lanes are jammed with car engines running, ruining the environment in the process.

Scottish Government Education Ministers; Fiona Hyslop MSP and Maureen Watt MSP. The SNP administration does not believe PPP education projects represent best value.

A central component of best value is Community Planning and Partnerships. The Local Government in Scotland Act 2003 placed local government as the key agency in the community planning process. It provided local authorities with a new 'power of well-being'.

A good example of such partnerships is "West Lothian Connected", which is a One Stop Shop operating from the Almondvale Centre in Livingston. A number of agencies, such as West Lothian Council, West Lothian Community Health and Care Partnership, NHS Lothian, JobcentrePlus, Victim Support, Careers Scotland and the Advice Shop are brought together under one roof.

Increasingly, local authorities are merging council departments to provide a more "holistic" service in the interests of best value. For example, it is rare these days for a local authority to have an "Education" department. It is accepted best practice that "education" is about more than what goes on in schools. Other agencies play a vital role in the well being of young people. Education is not just for young people. There are life-long learning opportunities provided by local authorities.

City of Edinburgh Council has a "Children and Families" department which brings together services such as adult education, child protection, childcare, children's residential care, community centres, fostering and adoption, under five services (nursery and children and family centres), primary, secondary

and special schools, services for children with disabilities, youth and justice work.

Are Public Private Partnerships (PPPS) best value? Many schools have been rebuilt or modernised through the use of Public Private Partnerships (PPPs).

PPPs mean that councils pay less now for improvements. A private company, or a consortium of private companies, is awarded the contract to build the school. Once completed, the local authority "rents" the school for a period, usually 30 years. During this period, the private company is responsible for maintenance and repairs. At the end of the agreed time, the local authority can choose to buy the school or continue to rent.

An advantage of PPP for a local authority is that it will know in advance how much its bills will be. There will be no unforeseen maintenance costs. Many secondary schools in Scotland were built in the early 1970s. These schools are now over thirty years old and in need of repair, upgrade or complete replacement. For a local authority such as Glasgow City Council, which has 29 secondary schools, the cost of repairing, upgrading or replacing its school stock would be substantial. The alternative to PPP might be to find the money now by raising Council Tax. But would this represent best value?

PPPs have been criticised for not offering "best value". Critics have claimed that, while cheaper in the short term, the eventual cost to the tax payer is much greater. Opponents of PPPs argue that local authorities should be given money by central government to upgrade schools. Alternatively, they argue local authorities should be given the option of borrowing the finance to improve schools.

How do we measure best value?

The Scottish Government monitors the drive for best value. It is the job of Audit Scotland's Accounts Commission to ensure local authorities deliver best value.

In 2005, Inverclyde Council was criticised by the Accounts Commission for its failure to provide best value, citing poor leadership and lack of accountability. Inverclyde Chief Executive Council Robert Cleary resigned, and in November 2005, the council was given a six month deadline to reorganise and improve.

Former Local Government Minister, Tom McCabe, reported "The people of Inverclyde expect and deserve the best possible public services. They also demand that their council is as efficient and effective as possible to allow it to deliver those services - the Executive shares that expectation with local people." In February 2007, Audit Scotland reported that Inverclyde Council had made many of the improvements suggested, but that there was still progress to be made.

COSLA's Improvement Service rewards local authority departments which have displayed excellence in their public services.

Activities

- Why might best value deliver a better quality of service for consumers?
- What is meant by the "holistic" delivery of local government services?
- What are the advantages and disadvantages of PPPs?
- How does the Scottish Government ensure best value is delivered by local authorities?

Financing Local Government

How we pay for our local services is the subject of heated debate. This concerns the "fairness", or otherwise, of the different possible systems of local government taxation. However, it also brings into question the financial relationship between the Scottish Government and the 32 Scottish local authorities.

At present, each Scottish local authority receives most of its funding, around 80%, from the Scottish Government. The remainder of the finance available to local authorities to pay for services is raised by Council Tax and local business rates. Each local authority can set its own rates of Council Tax and business tax.

The Labour opposition believes that, overall, Council Tax remains the fairest method of local taxation. Rather than end the Council Tax, it proposes to mend it, by changing the bandings, which have not been updated since 1990.

The SNP Government and the Scottish Liberal Democrats both prefer some form of Local Income Tax. A Local Income Tax would be based on the same principle as national income tax, although this is set by the Chancellor of the Exchequer at Westminster. Broadly speaking, the more a person earns in income, the more that person would pay in Local Income Tax.

The SNP's Local Income Tax differs significantly from the Scottish Liberal Democrats' plans. Some would say the SNP's Local Income Tax may not be a Local Income Tax at all.

It should be stated from the outset that no voter likes paying tax. Traditionally, any political party which promises to increase taxes, no matter how worthy the cause, loses votes. However, voters know that taxes are inevitable and they will pay taxes so long as they believe the tax to be "fair". What do "fair taxes" mean though?

In the late 1980s, Scottish voters rejected the Conservatives' Community Charge, or "poll tax" as it became known, because it was deemed to be "unfair". The poll tax had its advantages, but its "unfairness" lay in the fact that, more often than not, it was

35

"regressive". A regressive tax means that the richest pay proportionately less than the poorest.

In recent times, Scottish voters have preferred taxes that are "progressive". This means that the tax is based on the principle of the person's ability to pay. The more you earn, the more you pay. No Scottish political party's tax plans consciously depart from this principle. But all Scottish parties claim that their opponents' plans make poorer people pay proportionately more of their income in tax. Hence, their plans are "unfair".

The Burt Commission

The existing Council Tax is a property based tax. The higher the value of a person's property, the more that person pays in Council Tax to their local authority. Houses are valued within one of six bands, A-H, with H being the highest.

pushing them into more expensive Council Tax bands. But their actual disposable earnings are low, in relation to the amount of Council Tax they have to pay.

The Council Tax is not perfect. It is also unpopular. The 1999 – 2007 Labour-Liberal Democrat administrations realised this. In 2004, the Scottish Executive set up an independent commission, under the leadership of former Bank of Scotland boss, Sir Peter Burt, to look at alternatives to the Council Tax. The Burt Commission's report was published in November 2006.

The Labour Party, if not the Liberal Democrats, was pleased when Burt did not recommend replacing the Council Tax with a Local Income Tax. But, then First Minister Jack McConnell rejected Burt's support of a property based tax in which each homeowner should pay 1% of the property's value in annual Council Tax.

Given that the average Scottish property is worth £140,000, this would mean the average Scottish Council Tax bill would be £1,400 pounds. However, many parts of Scotland, especially Edinburgh and other affluent areas, have homes worth more than £140,000. It doesn't take a political or mathematical genius to work

The higher the value of a person's property, the more that person pays in Council Tax to their local authority.

Those who lose out financially from the Council Tax are those who have high value homes but who live on a fixed income. Typically, this means pensioners, whose homes have risen in value in recent years,

out that "middle Scotland", a key group of voters, would pay considerably more than £1400 per year. Middle Scotland is unlikely to be particularly well-disposed towards the politicians who introduce such a tax!

Scottish Labour's plans

Scottish Labour would rather re evaluate and re-band the original Council Tax bands of 1991. Many homes have risen in value a great deal since 1991, and the bands in many cases are very inaccurate. The bandings can be challenged. In some cases, individuals have won large rebates from local authorities as a result of being inaccurately banded. Labour promises to add two new Council Tax bands to the top and one at the bottom end of the scale. Labour also promises to cut the water and sewerage charges paid by pensioners. It estimates that a pensioner household in Council Tax Band D will be better off by £180 per year. Labour's opponents, however, claim that the reassessing of bands is a "secret tax bombshell". The Scottish Liberal Democrats claim Labour's Council Tax re-evaluation and re-banding would leave 59% of households worse off.

The Scottish Conservatives

The Scottish Conservatives are in favour of the Council Tax, but believe pensioners over the age of 65 should receive a 50% discount. This would not be means tested, and would be in addition to the discount a single pensioner already receives.

The Scottish Liberal Democrats

The Scottish Liberal Democrats plan an average local income tax rate of 3.625%. This is said to be based on the research of the Burt Commission, updated by recent work undertaken by the Institute of Fiscal Studies.

According to Scottish Liberal Democrat Finance spokesperson, George Lyon: "Local income tax is fair tax because it is based on ability to pay. This proposal is fair and fully costed. Local income tax will win new votes for the Liberal Democrats. Local income tax will remove the worry of rising council tax bills for those on low and fixed incomes. It will remove the worry and extra costs of a council tax re-valuation, which will take many houses up two or three bands, adding hundreds of pounds to bills."

The Scottish Liberal Democrats also claim Scottish Labour's Council Tax re-valuation and re-banding would leave 59% of households worse off, whereas Scottish Liberal Democrat plans would see the average family better off and half a million pensioners paying nothing.

SNP Government plans

The SNP are in control of the Scottish Government. It is the SNP's plans therefore that have generated the most heated responses. The SNP promises to replace the Council Tax with a "Local Income Tax", which would see tax payers pay an extra 3p in the pound A basic rate tax payer, who currently pays 20p in the pound income tax, would therefore pay a total of 23p in Local and UK Income Tax.

A higher rate tax payer, who currently pays 40%, would also pay an extra 3p in the pound as Local Income Tax. However, rather than being "local" to each of the 32 local authorities, "in the short to medium term", the 3p tax would apply equally across the whole of Scotland. During this period, Council Tax will be frozen at 2007-08 levels until the Local Income Tax is introduced.

The SNP claims that taxpayers on low and middle incomes will benefit by between £260 and £350 a year, and that only the top tenth of income earners will lose out. Only those who earn more than around £33,000 or £64,500 for a two-income couple would be worse off. According to Depute First Minister, Nicola Sturgeon, "This represents the biggest tax cut in a generation and is directed to particularly benefit pensioners and middle Scotland." Unsurprisingly, Labour has been quick to criticise the plan.

Strip away the party political spin and what advantages do Council Tax and Local Income Tax have?

"Not only have the SNP completely removed local discretion in the setting of tax, they are now reintroducing elements of Margaret Thatcher's poll tax, in that every worker in a household will now pay this tax."
Tom McCabe MSP, former Labour Finance Minister

The Council Tax is, to some extent, based on an ability to pay. For most people, pensioners excepted, the ability to afford a home is an indication of their wealth. Those who can afford high value homes tend to buy high value homes, and those who cannot, do not.

The advantage of Council Tax is that it is relatively easy to collect. A tax is no good if people can avoid paying it! Figures vary across the local authorities, but, in recent years, Council Tax collection rates have improved. People can move around the country, but houses can't. Those on low incomes are also entitled to Council Tax benefit. Social Security is a reserved Westminster power. Both Labour and Conservatives have plans to help those, such as pensioners, who are not entitled to Council Tax benefit, but are on fixed incomes.

But the Council Tax is unpopular. After mortgage payments, the Council Tax, is, for many families, the second biggest household expense. Nor is there any link between payment for services and how fequently services are used, if at all. High income families who may not use certain local authority services, such as social work or social housing, may resent paying large bills to cover these services they rarely use.

From a less self interested viewpoint, Council Tax does not proportionately take into account differences in wealth. A person earning over £100,000 per year may well pay more in Council Tax, but he/she may not. There is no guarantee that person will live in a high band property. Even if he/she does, the high income Council Tax payer may only pay a small proportion more

> "Our Local Income Tax plans represent the biggest tax cut in a generation and is directed to particularly benefit pensioners and middle Scotland."
> Nicola Sturgeon MSP

in Council Tax than, for example, someone earning £20,000 per year.

Nicola Surgeon MSP (SNP), Glasgow Govan.

Council Tax hits those with low incomes but expensive houses. Pensioners are hit especially hardest. Pensioners may well have "wealth" in the shape of the value of their home, but this is "paper wealth". The only way they can access this wealth is to sell their home!

To some extent, Local Income Tax solves the problem of redistributing wealth. Those with higher incomes pay more. Its supporters argue that as Scotland has more middle income earners the majority of Scots would benefit from a Local Income Tax through our small number of very high earners paying more.

But, critics of Local Income Tax, such as Sir Peter Burt, point to the administrative burden of collecting Local Income Tax. The Scottish Parliament does not have the power to force HM Revenue and Customs to collect Local Income Tax at the same time as it deducts Income Tax from people's salaries. Employers would have to register employees in their local authority area and payroll staff may, in theory, have to apply different rates of Local Income Tax to employees living in different local authorities. All this costs money.

Burt estimates it would cost the Scottish Parliament up to £55m. Some companies may move to England to avoid the inconvenience and cost.
In addition, what happens to Council Tax benefit? Currently the poorest receive Council Tax benefit. Some Scots pay no Council Tax at all. Council Tax benefit is the responsibility of the UK Parliament

But, if a Local Income Tax was introduced, those on lowest incomes could lose their Council Tax benefit. According to Professor David Bell of Stirling University, "That's the killer for local income tax. Unless it is introduced on a UK basis, there is an enormous problem over council tax benefit."

The debate will go on. Ultimately, in a democracy the people will decide which form of taxation is fairest. We may not like paying taxes, but we need local services. We do not know, as yet, how successful the minority SNP Government will be in passing its policies on a Local Income Tax. Given that the Liberal Democrats favour a version of a Local Income Tax, common ground may be found. But if Labour, Green and Conservative MSPs oppose a Local Income Tax, we may be in for gridlock.

Activities

- Explain how the Council Tax works.
- Why does Scottish Labour support the Council Tax?
- Why does the Scottish Government seek to abolish the Council Tax?
- What are the advantages and disadvantages of the Scottish Government's proposed Local Income Tax?

Revision

Some students find it helpful to revise via mp3 files rather than, or as well as, text books. If so, the modernityeducation podcasts are ideal.

If so, please visit www.modernityeducation.co.uk

You can download the first series of Modernitypodcasts, Modern UK Politics, which have been produced to complement this text book.

Each podcast lasts between 12-15 minutes and addresses the key issues in each Study Theme of Political Issues in the United Kingdom.

Series One Modern UK Politics

1 The First Past the Post Voting System

2 The Additional Member System

3 The Single Transferable Vote and Democracy

4 Voting Behaviour in the UK

5 The Influence of the Media on Elections

6 Relations between Holyrood and Westminster

7 Powers of the Modern Prime Minister

8 The Labour Party – Continuity and Change

9 Pressure Groups and their Methods

10 Party Politics in Scotland.

T h e   B i g   P i c t u r e

All Prime Ministers like to be seen as having "a vision". Margaret Thatcher's vision was to create a "property owning democracy". John Major sought to restore "decency" to British life. Tony Blair championed "New Labour, New Britain". Gordon Brown is attempting to create "a new politics".

Gordon Brown has taken over government at a time when public disillusionment with politics is at an all time high. Voting turnouts are down. Opinion polls show that the public resents the over-use of "spin" by politicians. Constitutionally, there has been criticism of the powers enjoyed by the UK Prime Minister.

Tony Blair's so-called "government by sofa", where the Prime Minister decided government policy along with a handful of non-elected special advisers and spin doctors, rather than the Cabinet, has been criticised. Not only by the Conservatives. predictably, but also by the Butler Report into the decisions leading up to the war in Iraq. Lord Butler uses civil service vocabulary, but his conclusions are clear enough; Tony Blair re-wrote British constitutional tradition and concentrated power in the hands of himself and his most trusted allies:

"We are concerned that the informality and circumscribed character of the government's procedures, which we saw in the context of policy-making towards Iraq, risks reducing the scope for informed collective political judgment"

Pressure groups have called for the House of Lords to be directly elected on a national/regional basis.

They would like the Prime Minister to be stripped of powers, such as the right to decide the date of a General Election (brought into sharp focus in October 2007, when Gordon Brown famously bungled his planned early General Election) and the right to declare war. The emergence of an SNP Government in Scotland has raised the constitutional position of the West Lothian question and the rights of MPs from Scotland, including, of course, the Prime Minister himself, to vote on legislation which only exists in England and Wales.

The rapid development of new technologies has also changed the way pressure groups work and the relationships pressure groups have with government. The days when government policy was decided over "beer and sandwiches" by Ministers, trade unions and business leaders are long gone. Today, Ministers have a dialogue, not just with the traditional insider groups, but with Citizen Juries and online communities. In the immediate aftermath of the non-election of November 2007, Gordon Brown faced a difficult time during Prime Minister's Question Time. Attempting to come back off the ropes, after Conservative taunts that the Prime Minister had "lost his bottle", the Prime Minister claimed that only a handful of people had signed the petition for an election on the Downing Street web site. Twenty-four hours later, five thousand had signed the petition.

It is clear that decision making in central government is likely to undergo considerable change in the years to come.

Chapter 4 Governing the UK

Powers of the Prime Minister

Prime Minister Gordon Brown

The Prime Minister and the Cabinet are usually described as "the Executive". Several political analysts have claimed that, with the exception of John Major's years (1991-1997), the Premierships of Margaret Thatcher and Tony Blair saw the Prime Minister dominate the Cabinet. Partly because these Prime Ministers had such large majorities in the House of Commons, it has been argued that parliamentary government has been replaced by "Prime Ministerial" Government. Some even claim that we now have a "Presidential" Prime Minister.

Unlike the USA, the UK does not have a written constitution which details the powers of elected representatives. As such, Liberal Prime Minister Herbert Asquith (1908-1916) described the powers of Prime Minister as "what the office holder chooses and is able to make of it". Different Prime Ministers have different styles of leadership and have, therefore, exercised their powers in different ways. Any Prime Minister has a wide range of formal and informal powers.

First Among Equals

Traditionally, the British Prime Minister is primus inter pares, first among equals. Unlike the USA President, the UK Prime Minister is not directly elected as Prime Minister. The Prime Minister is elected as a constituency Member of Parliament. However, as leader of the governing political party, the Prime Minister heads a Cabinet team of Government Ministers.

The Prime Minister appoints this team and can sack or re-shuffle Ministers whenever he/she chooses. Most MPs are ambitious. They would like to be in the Cabinet and realise that, as well as political talent, proven loyalty to the Prime Minister is the passport to the Executive.

The Prime Minister will promote trusted colleagues, but also political rivals, who would be too powerful outside the Cabinet. Tony Blair had to make Gordon Brown Chancellor of the Exchequer as he was too powerful an adversary to be left out.

Within the Cabinet, there is seniority in status. Chancellor of Exchequer is a much sought after position. Likewise, Foreign or Home Secretary carries a prestige other Cabinet posts do not have. Cabinet Ministers are ambitious too. Most Prime Ministers operate an informal "inner Cabinet" of most trusted Ministers. Again, loyalty to the Prime Minister is usually rewarded. Disloyalty is punished.

The doctrine of "collective responsibility" is used to provide the Prime Minister with authority over the Cabinet. Once a collective decision is reached in Cabinet, all Ministers must publicly support it. If a Minister feels he cannot support Government policy, he/she must resign. Robin Cook, famously, resigned from the Cabinet over the Blair Government handling of the war in Iraq. Resignation from Cabinet can often mean the end of an MP's promotion prospects and is a big step to take. The Prime Minister can use the doctrine of collective responsibility to command loyalty and compliance.

The Prime Minister is responsible for preparing the agenda of Cabinet meetings. Contentious items, or items the Prime Minister does not wish to have discussed, can be omitted. Tony Blair's Cabinet meetings were famously short.

Patronage

The UK has an honours system whereby individuals are recognised and rewarded for merit, bravery, achievement or services to the country. Many business leaders value a seat in the House of Lords for the prestige and business opportunities it brings. Experienced MPs also look forward to a life peerage in the House of Lords, as it prolongs their political life.

The Prime Minister controls many of these honours. Each year the party leaders can nominate a certain number of new peers to the House of Lords. Tony Blair famously appointed many of his supporters, the so-called "Tony's cronies", to the House of Lords. The Prime Minister claimed this was to counteract the Conservatives' large majority in the House of Lords.

Tony Blair was accused, and cleared, of selling peerages after four businessmen who gave Labour £4.5m in unpublicised loans, were subsequently nominated for peerages. This became known as the "Cash for Honours" scandal. Gordon Brown has come under criticism for "cronyism" by appointing Jack McConnell, instead of a civil servant to the post of High Commissioner for Malawi.

Leader of the Party

As we have seen, many MPs are loyal to the Prime Minister through self-interest. They seek promotion, and loyalty can be rewarded. However, most MPs support the Prime Minister because they agree with him. He is their leader and the person the public associate with their party. What is good for the Prime Minister is good for the Prime Minister's MPs. The opposite is the case too. Back bench rebellions damage the party in opinion polls. The public does not like parties which are divided. Thus, the Prime Minister can use appeals for party unity to his advantage.

The Prime Minister manages MPs' voting behaviour through the Whip System. The Government Chief Whip is directly answerable to the Prime Minister. He/she attends the Cabinet and makes the day-to-day arrangements for the Government's business programme.

Whips have an important role in party business within Parliament, particularly when the Government has a small majority. For major votes it is vital for government and opposition to maximise the turnout, and the Whips try to ensure that every MP from their party turns out to vote.

'Three-line whips' are imposed on important occasions, such as second readings of significant Bills and motions of no confidence.

Failure by MPs to attend a vote with a three-line

whip is usually seen as a rebellion against the party and may eventually result in disciplinary action, such as suspension from the parliamentary party.

Dictate the media agenda

The Prime Minister makes news. He dictates the media's agenda. If he decides to make a state visit or make policy announcements, the media will follow. Tony Blair had a love/hate relationship with the media. He described the UK media as "feral beasts". Yet, no other Prime Minister has been as skilled at the black arts of spin and news management.

Gordon Brown appears to be no slouch. While his rival David Cameron has a constant battle to achieve positive media coverage, Prime Minister Brown can attend United Nations summits or meet with foreign heads of states. His constant media profile creates an impression among voters of a political heavyweight. The Prime Minister can always be on the offensive, while opposition politicians need to wait for his mistakes before they pounce.

Decide the date of the General Election

It is often said that Oppositions do not win elections, governments lose them. Within a five year period, the Prime Minister has the power to call General Elections. This will usually be when the party is doing well in opinion polls and opposition parties are struggling. In the run up to a General Election, favourable economic conditions can be created and popular decisions can be made.

Gordon Brown's premiership has been a fascinating case study of this power. As Chancellor he handed decisions over interest rates, a key lever of economic policy, to the Bank of England. New Labour hoped this move would rebut any charges that it was "playing politics" with the economy. Yet, in September 2007, only 100 days into his term as Prime Minister, Gordon Brown set in motion speculation that he was about to call a General Election. It was only the Conservatives' unveiling of a new tax policy, on inheritance tax, and the party's subsequent climb in the opinion polls, that made the Prime Minister change his mind on an early General Election. Within days, Labour had adopted almost the same tax plan as the Conservatives!

Activities

- Explain what is meant by Herbert Asquith's statement.
- To what extent is the Prime Minister "first among equals"?
- Sum up the powers all UK Prime Ministers have at their disposal

Margaret Thatcher

Margaret Thatcher was Prime Minister from 1979-1990. The so-called iron lady, she had a "one of us" style of government. She used the Prime Ministerial power of patronage very effectively. Her parliamentary colleagues knew acquiescence was the way to promotion. She appointed her supporters, such as Norman Tebbit and Cecil Parkinson, to key positions in the Cabinet. She was ruthless with those who did not share her convictions.

In 1979-80, she sacked 12 Cabinet Ministers. She reduced the frequency of Cabinet meetings. She enforced "collective responsibility" on her colleagues, but, at the same time, publicly criticised "weak" Ministers by briefing against them to the media. She left key items off the Cabinet agenda; an issue which her rival, Michael Heseltine, claimed was the reason for his resignation.

Ultimately, her style of leadership brought her downfall. The decision to pursue policies, particularly the Poll Tax, which did not have Cabinet and parliamentary support, never mind the support of the public, forced the Conservatives' 1922 Committee, the famous "men in grey suits", to ask for her resignation. One by one, her Cabinet colleagues turned against her. She described their actions as "treachery with a smile".

The experience of Margaret Thatcher shows that there are limits on the power of a Prime Minister. Prime Ministers are usually driven individuals, who can seek change. But if this change steps outside the approval of the wider parliamentary party, and public opinion, the Prime Minister will be held accountable.

John Major

When the Conservatives forced Margaret Thatcher's resignation, they sought a less confrontational leader. Consequently, John Major's style was more consensus seeking. He sought more collective Cabinet decision making.

He did though lead a party which was very divided, over Europe in particular, but also, in the aftermath of Margaret Thatcher, divided over the political direction the party should be taking. Major was plotted against by members of his Cabinet. Major famously described them as "bastards". John Major lost the 1997 General Election to Tony Blair's New Labour. The Conservatives became embroiled in in-fighting as well as political and personal "sleaze". Public opinion desired a change. Things, as the song went, could only get better.

Tony Blair

Tony Blair was a quite remarkable Prime Minister. He was a strong leader who was prepared to use his constitutional and personal powers to stamp his authority over the Cabinet and Parliament.

Blair was an admirer of Margaret Thatcher's dynamism and leadership. There are many comparisons. He too reduced the frequency and length of Cabinet meetings. He too appointed supporters to key positions. He had large parliamentary majorities and a supportive

parliamentary party to drive through legislation.
He did though have to keep his political opponent,
Gordon Brown, in the Cabinet as Chancellor of the
Exchequer. Like Margaret Thatcher over the poll tax,
a defining single issue, the Iraq war, lost Blair his
popularity with the public and his political party.

Activities

- To what extent did the experience of
  Margaret Thatcher show that there are
  limits to Prime Ministerial power?
- Why was John Major a very different Prime
  Minister from Margaret Thatcher?
- What similarities were there in the leadership
  styles of Margaret Thatcher and Tony Blair?

Tony Blair and Sofa Government

The phrase "sofa government", coined by Lord
Butler, has been used to describe Tony Blair's
relations with Cabinet and Parliament. Margaret
Thatcher, who also had little time for long drawn out
Cabinet discussions, also enjoyed a "government by
sofa".
When asked why she kept inviting a businessman,
David Hart, to Downing Street, she replied, "Because
he upsets the civil servants".

Elected in 1997 on a "modernising" agenda, Tony
Blair and his inner circle were suspicious of the
machinery of government. They were in a hurry to
transform the country. They believed that senior civil
servants would stifle the drive of the Blair revolution.
Key decisions were made by trusted allies outside of
Cabinet meetings, over a coffee and emails.

> "The Blair government sought to circumvent the civil service through the use of Special Advisers and consultants on an unprecedented scale"
>
> Max Hastings.

The Special Advisers appointed by Blair were
not industry experts or those with specialist
knowledge. They were news management
professionals, or "spin doctors", as they
are usually known. Tony Blair's closest
colleagues, Alastair Campbell and Jonathan
Powell, were political appointees, not elected
politicians. Whilst there have been Special
Advisers employed by Governments in the
past, their numbers increased by a huge
amount under Tony Blair. Tony Blair
had 29, mainly in the Downing Street
Policy Directorate and his Strategic
Communications Unit.

Jo Moore is, perhaps, the Special Adviser most
widely known to the public. In 2001, she infamously
suggested that the events of 9/11 made it a good day
to publish Government "bad news". Following her
resignation, a special civil service commission was set
up to monitor the role of special advisers.

On Iraq, Tony Blair bypassed the Cabinet, sharing
discussions with Campbell or Powell, even President
Bush, rather than his Cabinet or parliamentary
colleagues. When he did speak to cabinet colleagues,
these conversations took the form of "bilaterals",
one-to-one meetings, rather than minuted, collective
Cabinet debate.

The Butler report (2004) on the intelligence provided
on weapons of mass destruction in Iraq, was critical
of the "informality and circumscribed character" of
Tony Blair's policy-making.

Conservative leader, David Cameron, would seek to limit the number of special advisers and limit Prime Ministerial power over going to war, giving MPs in the House of Commons the decision-making power.

Executive Power and Parliament

There are constitutional opportunities for Parliament to scrutinise the Executive.

Votes in the House of Commons

Jacqui Smith MP was Tony Blair's Chief Whip for most of the 2001-2005 Parliament. She had a key role in ensuring that the Executive had its legislation passed in the House of Commons.

Backbench MPs can rebel. All governments will have a hard core of MPs who are not "on message". Tony Blair's 1997-2001 Government was much more united than its Conservative predecessor and there were few dissenters from the "Blair project".

When Tony Blair's majority was cut from 162 to 66 in 2005, the balance of power shifted away from the Prime Minister towards parliament. The Executive was defeated for the first time over plans to introduce 90 day detention for terrorist suspects.

By 2006, Tony Blair had to rely on Conservative MPs to have his education bill passed. When Tony Blair announced his intention to stand down as Prime Minister, he lost his authority over back benchers. There were further acts of defiance over welfare reform and foundation hospitals and over the war in Iraq, the biggest Commons rebellion since the repeal of the Corn Laws in the 19th century.

Prime Minister's Question Time

Tony Blair changed Prime Minister's Question Time to one weekly half-hour slot, rather than two fifteen minute per week. This allowed him to prepare better and more accurately anticipate Opposition attacks.

Prime Minister's Question Time is the one piece of Parliament activity which the public tends to see on teatime news. It is highly theatrical. It doesn't change policy, but it can improve or damage party morale.

A Prime Minister, or Opposition party leader who is in command at Prime Minister's Question Time, can raise the spirits of MPs and party supporters, motivating them to campaign better in the country at large. Conversely, a poor Prime Ministerial performance at Question Time can dampen party morale. Prime Ministers, who can show dominance in the House of Commons, find it easier to achieve party unity and also prolong their life as Prime Minister.

Select Committees

Parliament has both Standing and Ad Hoc committees which scrutinise government legislation. The committees have the power to call witnesses and documents, but cannot force MPs or Ministers to attend. Most MPs do so, however, as refusal to attend or answer questions will not look good. Committees produce a report, which sometimes gains public attention, but mostly does not. Select committees often act as a magnet for pressure groups, but rarely change the overall direction of policy. Membership of select committees reflects party strength, so are therefore dominated by government MPs.

Recently the House of Commons has formed a "Liaison Committee". The Liaison Committee is composed of the chairs of all the various committees. It attempts to speak for the Commons as a whole, rather than from a partisan party political point of view. Tony Blair offered to appear before this committee, and did so, to deflect criticism that he had been neglecting parliament.

House of Commons inquiries

There were four separate inquiries into the pre-war intelligence on Iraq. Tony Blair survived all four parliamentary inquiries into his actions. In each one, he had to defend himself in the Commons, and in the media too. Critics may say that the reports were "whitewashes" and did not ask the right questions. Tony Blair survived them all.

Adam Price MP. The Plaid Cymru MP alleged that Prime Minister Tony Blair broke constitutional principles over the war in Iraq.

Why? That great rule of politics in all democracies. The economy, stupid!! During Tony Blair's terms in office, most voters in the UK felt good about their financial prospects. So why change? As opposition leader, David Cameron has to offer a significantly better vision, and much more appealing policies than Gordon Brown, in order to win.

Opposition Days

These are days set aside for Opposition parties to criticise aspects of government policy. While there is little possibility of the Government actually changing policy on the issues which are tabled, opposition parties can use this forum to embarrass the Executive. SNP back bench MP Angus MacNeil pursued Lord Levy and Tony Blair over the "cash for peerages" scandal. Adam Price, Plaid Cymru MP attempted to revive a parliamentary procedure to impeach Tony Blair over the Iraq war.

The House of Lords

Peers in the House of Lords are unelected. This appears to make them more independent and willing to challenge the Executive. The fact that many of these men (they are mostly men) have already served a political career also makes them less likely to be influenced by promises of jobs from the Prime Minister.

In the 2001-2005 Parliament, the Government was defeated in the Lords 245 times. Following defeat in the Lords, bills return to the Commons in what is known as "parliamentary ping pong". It is claimed that this process of scrutiny improves the quality of legislation. Peers in Lords have more time than Commons MPs to examine legislation.

Events

When former Prime Minister, Harold Macmillan (1957-1963), was asked by a young journalist what can most easily steer a government off course, he replied "Events, dear boy, events."

In short, politics is unpredictable.

The kind of issues which are high on the political agenda these days are issues which do not sit easily as party political ones. Terrorism? Religious hatred? Climate change? Family breakdown? There is no clear Government "line" on these issues the way there was in the more straightforward Left v Right days of old. Many Labour MPs can feel that they have more in common with Liberal Democrat, or even Conservative, MPs on these issues than they have with their party colleagues. The opportunities for MPs to rebel are therefore greater. MPs who choose to defy the party whips can have "fifteen minutes of fame" with the "feral beasts" (© Tony Blair) of the 24/7 news media who thrive on political dissent.

Activities

- Sum up the main constitutional constraints on Prime Ministerial power.
- Why were there few parliamentary rebellions in the early days of the Blair governments?
- Why did rebellions increase in later years?
- Why might MPs rebel against their political party more easily in modern times?
- Which parliamentary opportunity do you feel is the most effective in controlling a Prime Minister?

The Civil Service and Government

Tony Blair enjoyed using Special Advisers. Special Advisers are an additional resource for a Minister. They provide assistance from a standpoint that is more politically committed than that provided by the Civil Service. Special Advisers are often described as "spin doctors". A large part of their job is to manipulate news so that the Government is perceived by the public in its most positive light.

The Conservatives' "Democracy taskforce" has criticised Tony Blair's "sofa government". Ken Clarke concluded that "Cabinet government has been all but destroyed. Most ministers have become little more than the presentational vehicles for the policies of political appointees in Number Ten. Presentation has led policy. The Civil Service has been left to carry the blame for policies that have proved impossible to implement".

Most people's view of civil servants is coloured by the famous television comedy "Yes Minister". An ongoing theme of the series is the way in which devious Civil Servants manipulate gullible Government Ministers. Ministers are, after all, here today, gone tomorrow. Civil Servants work in Government departments for much longer. Ministers have many different demands on their time and energies. Hence, they place great trust on their team of Ministers for reliable information. Civil Servants, perhaps based in the one department for a length of time, have considerable expertise in that policy area.

According to the Yes Minister model, Civil Servants do not trust Ministers, who may have different, shorter term political priorities. So, they devise ways of making sure the Minister chooses options the Civil Service agrees with. All of this, if true, is highly undemocratic. Ministers, however wise or foolish, are elected by the people.

The most senior Civil Servants traditionally come from elitist social class backgrounds. It is claimed that they have an inbuilt bias in favour of "conservative" solutions. The Yes Minister view of the Civil Service may contain a degree of truth, but it does not do justice to the complexity of relations at play in government. It wouldn't be a very funny programme if it did! There may well be bumbling, easily duped Ministers, and there may well be devious

Civil Servants, but in the vast majority of cases, Ministers and Civil Servants work together with common goals. The relationship is one of "mutual dependency".

The Scottish Government at Victoria Quay, Edinburgh

The Civil Service Code

The Civil Service is referred to as the Home Civil Service. Civil Servants have to work within strict rules, known as the Civil Service Code. The Civil Service Code sets out the constitutional framework within which all Civil Servants work and the values they are expected to uphold.

Civil Servants are servants of the Crown. The constitutional and practical role of the Civil Service is to assist the UK Government at Westminster, the Scottish Government at Holyrood, the National Assembly for Wales in Cardiff and the Northern Ireland Assembly at Stormont, with integrity, honesty, impartiality and objectivity.

Civil Servants should not misuse their official position or information acquired in the course of their official duties to further their private interests or those of others. They should not receive benefits of any kind from a third party which might reasonably be seen to compromise their personal judgment or integrity.

The Civil Service in Scotland remains part of the Home Civil Service. However, Civil Servants who work for the Scottish Government owe their loyalty to the devolved administration rather than the UK Government. Scottish Government Civil Servants are accountable to Scottish Ministers, who are themselves accountable to the Scottish Parliament.

Relations between Ministers and Civil Servants

The job of a Minister, for example, The Minister for Work and Pensions, is to be accountable for Government policies in these areas. A good Minister will have a long-term vision of employment and pension issues and be aware of current debates and controversies. However, he/she may have arrived from a non-employment background and have no specific expertise in these areas. Work and Pensions is an enormous Government department whose decisions affect just about everyone in the UK. But the Minister will make an effort to "get on top of the brief", by speaking to trusted colleagues and practitioners and also "insider" pressure groups. He/she will, of course, also rely on the advice and expertise of the Civil Servants in the Department for Work and Pensions.

The role of the Civil Service is to advise the Minister on how best to implement the policies the Minister and the Cabinet has decided upon. In other words, it is not up to the Civil Servant to decide these policies, but to offer advice on their successful implementation.

Hazel Blears MP. Secretary of State for Communities and Local Government. Ms Blears will depend on her team of civil servants for policy advice.

In reality, the relationship becomes one of mutual dependence. The Minister is surrounded by many experts within the Civil Service. In time, the Minister will know which Civil Servants he/she can trust to provide expert, accurate, up-to-date information. In turn, Civil Servants want to see "their" Minister succeed. There is a professional pride in seeing policies succeed and life for the public improve. Civil Servants receive promotion based on performance. The ability to support Ministers with high quality advice and information is the key to promotion. A Civil Servant who can display expertise

in the qualities of the Civil Service Code is a Civil Servant on the way to the top. A Civil servant who was disloyal to a Minister, or other colleagues in the departmental team, would not receive promotion, and could in fact be disciplined.

A good example is when the Minister speaks in a parliamentary debate. Civil Servants will prepare their Minister for the debate. They will perhaps draft a speech. They will make the Minister aware of likely "points of attack" by the opposition and arm the Minister with facts and figures to rebut the opposition case.

In the case of media management, a vital aspect of modern politics, Civil Servants will prepare news releases for television, press and radio. They will "spin" information in such a way as to project the best possible image of the Minister's work and direct attention to areas where the Minister has made most progress.

Civil Servants who support the Prime Minister have an even more responsible job. One of the main responsibilities of the Prime Minister is to answer questions put to him in the House of Commons at

Prime Minister's Question Time

Opposition MPs, can ask supplementary questions on any aspect of Government policy. It could be about health care. But it could be about drugs policy, nuclear power, housing, or whatever the opposition feels it can gain most political capital from. Prime Minister's Question Time is the most high-profile of all the Commons procedures. Since cameras have been allowed in the chamber and events televised, it has become increasingly theatrical. A good performance by the Prime Minister can raise Government morale. A bad one can lead to low opinion poll ratings and questions over leadership.

It is the job of the Prime Minister's team of civil servants and special advisers to anticipate the topic of questions. They try to equip him with statistics and political arguments to answer the questions well and avoid political defeat. As such, the image of Sir Humphrey in Yes Minister is quite wide of the mark. The relationship between Minister and Civil Service is rarely exploitative, but symbiotic, where one supports the other.

A Minister with drive and competence will motivate Civil Servants to work better and more efficiently. A Minister with a talented Civil Service team behind him will be a better politician. By contrast, opposition politicians do not have the support of the machinery of Government. They must prepare for parliamentary debates, such as Prime Ministers Question Time, with only the support of party researchers. While talented and enthusiastic, researchers are usually young and inexperienced. Opposition Ministers lack the high quality support which the Government has at its disposal. Ministers have the whole of the Government's agencies, researchers, advisers and thousands of salaried staff to provide them with information.

The Civil Service is criticised by both the political Left and Right. For the Left, socialists view senior Civil Servants as, at best, conservative with a small 'c', and, at worst, Conservative with a big 'C'. They believe that their backgrounds, normally from the elite schools and universities, take them away from the concerns of "normal" people. At times the Left believes their bias may be calculated, for example advising against policies which help "undeserving" poorer people, but the Left suspects more often it is likely to be unconscious. Because their personal lives and social contacts are so divorced from the lives of the socially excluded, senior Civil Service advice may be coloured by "middle class" attitudes and expectations.

The Right distrusts the Civil Service too. They feel that the Civil Service is unwilling to consider private sector solutions. Conservatives sometimes claim the Civil Service has a vested interest in raising taxes and spending money in the public sector to preserve their own jobs and careers. The Right believes the Civil Service lacks dynamism and is inefficient. Right wingers would like to see more people from business and the private sector brought in to advise Ministers.

Special Advisers

Special Advisers are employed to help Ministers on matters where the work of Government and the work of the Government Party overlap and it would be inappropriate for permanent civil servants to become involved. They are an additional source for the Minister, providing advice from a standpoint that is more politically committed and politically aware than would be available to a Minister from the Civil Service.

A large part of their job is to "spin" (not lie, there is a subtle difference!) news to the media and the Government in the most positive light. Special Advisers are temporary civil servants appointed under Article 3 of the Civil Service Order. They are exempt from the general requirement that civil servants should be appointed on merit, and behave with political impartiality and objectivity, so that they may retain the confidence of future governments of a different political complexion.

As such, there is a strong overlap between their Government work and their party political work. Only a very loyal party member, one who is completely "on message" with the Government, will be employed as a Special Adviser. A Special Adviser's appointment ends at the end of the administration which appointed him/her. The responsibility for the management and conduct of Special Advisers, including discipline, rests with the Minister who made the appointment.

The work of Special Advisers was made infamous with the case of Jo Moore. As Special Adviser to the then Transport Secretary, Stephen Byers, Jo Moore sent an email which badly back-fired. She stated that September 11 2001, the day of the al-Qaeda attacks on the USA, was "a very good day to get out anything we want to bury". Jo Moore's message was timed at 1455 BST on 11 September, within an hour of the second plane flying into the World Trade Center, but before either tower collapsed. Jo Moore was forced to resign after widespread condemnation of her actions.

Commentators have asked what other controversial items of news have been "buried" during other national emergencies. It is unlikely the traditional Civil Service could be manipulated by Ministers in this way. New Labour has been strongly criticised for undermining the traditional role of the Civil Service through its reliance on Special Advisers.

Activities

- What is the stereotypical image of Civil Servants, as portrayed in Yes Minister?
- Why is this portrayal inaccurate?
- In what ways do Civil Servants assist Government Ministers?
- Why is the Civil Service criticised by both the political right and the left?
- Why did the Jo Moore case bring negative publicity to the role of Special Advisers?

Interview with David Mundell

David Mundell is Conservative MP for Dumfriesshire, Clydesdale and Tweeddale. He is Shadow Secretary of State for Scotland.

Modernity: What opportunities do opposition MPs have to influence the Executive?

David Mundell: It all depends on the majority the Government has. If the government majority is small, opposition and back bench government MPs have much more scope for influence. The current Labour Government is now much easier to influence because its majority is smaller. The same was true for the 1992-97 Conservative Government, because of the tighter majority it had.

Opposition MPs can create a media campaign around certain issues. They can make amendments to legislation at committee stages of bills. They can also pursue Private Members Bills, although these are a small part of the legislative programme of the House of Commons.

MPs from Scotland can achieve amendments on Standing Committees such as the Scottish Affairs Committee. The House of Lords often picks up on an amendment which a committee has recommended. The amendments to the identity cards legislation is a good example.

Modernity: Is the Prime Minister too powerful?

David Mundell: We need to redefine the powers of Parliament and give it more strength. Our parliamentary system works best when Governments don't have too big a majority. There needs to be a re-balancing of executive power, to allow Parliament greater scrutiny.

We've moved to a more presidential style which has been driven by the media and public desire for

celebrity. Brown v Cameron is likely to be the way the next General Election is conducted. Parliament has lost out, and we need to examine how the Executive can be better held to account. Tony Blair had an informal style of decision making with no formal record of how key decisions were taken. This lack of structure is unacceptable.

Modernity: Given the existence of a First Minister in the Scottish Parliament speaking for Scotland, what is the role of the Secretary of State for Scotland?

David Mundell: The role is no doubt different because of the creation of the Scottish Parliament. The formal relationships never properly developed because the same party essentially was in power in both parliaments. The debate on the role of the Secretary of State for Scotland is only now taking place. Mechanisms for the day to day relationships will have to begin. There is quite a pivotal role for the Secretary of State for Scotland in managing relations between the two Governments.

Modernity: How do you feel the West Lothian Question can be resolved?

David Mundell: It's not going to go away, it can't be ignored. There is a general feeling of unfairness. I could vote to ban smoking in England, but not in my own constituency.

Matters that are purely to do with England should be dealt with only by English MPs. I don't think there's any real mood in England to have an English Parliament or English regional government. The answer lies within the structures of the House of Commons to have an English Grand Committee, composed of MPs from English constituencies, to deal with English-only issues.

Modernity: What is your parliamentary role as an MP?

David Mundell: Most of my work is done behind the scenes. I deal with a lot of constituency business. I'm heavily involved in trying to improve services to Lockerbie station, as many of the trains are on their way to and from England. I recently took part in an Adjournment Debate on fishing rights on the River Esk, which is a cross-border river. I also led a debate on the conduct of the Scottish parliament elections which were not conducted in a way anyone would have wanted. The Scotland Office has responsibility for Scottish Parliament elections.

The Role of the House of Lords

There are around 746 members of the House of Lords. None are elected. Most are appointees by the Prime Minister. Some are "hereditary" peers, i.e. their seat in the Lords has been passed down the family. Up to 12 law lords also sit in the Lords. Their

main work lies not in debates, but in judging cases.

The House of Lords is the highest appeal court in the UK. There are also 26 Church of England archbishops and bishops, who can speak and vote in the Lords. Some peers rarely show up. It is perfectly possible to check in to the House of Lords, claim up to £320 per day in expenses, and walk out again. Disgraced peers, such as Mike Watson (Lord Watson of Invergowrie), who has spent time in jail for arson, retain their seat in the Lords. The same applies to Conrad Black (Baron Black of Crossharbour) who, in 2007, was found guilty in the USA of fraud.

It took until the 20th century for all men and women over 18 to be given the right to vote. Up until the 20th century, the Lords had almost as much power as the House of Commons. Sometimes the Prime Minister and Cabinet colleagues were members of the Lords rather than the Commons. When the vote was extended to all, the Commons felt that the Lords did not have a democratic mandate to block laws passed by those elected by the people. Reform of the House of Lords has been on the political agenda for a century. Yet, even in its current unelected format, the House of Lords still has its supporters.

A check on the power of the Executive

Margaret Thatcher won large Commons majorities in 1983 and 1987; Tony Blair has won two - in 1997 and 2001 and had a commanding majority in 2005. The power of the Whips in the Commons means the possibilities of an "elected dictatorship" are strong. Remember too that Tony Blair's 2005 Government won only 35% of the popular vote. Should there not be some procedure for checking the power of the Executive, no matter how archaic or imperfect?

If it is near impossible for the official Opposition to defeat the Government in the Commons, the House of Lords' role becomes crucial. The Lords is there to protect minorities who might otherwise be steamrollered by the majority - and it's also there to protect the government from itself, to revise bad legislation before it becomes law.

While peers have political party affiliations, they tend to be less partisan than MPs in the Commons. They have more time to consider legislation than the hurried Commons does. It is argued that the experience of peers, and their opportunity to discuss laws in a less party-politically biased way (they do not have to worry about being re-elected), means that legislation can be, and has been, improved by their input.

Why reform the Lords?

New Labour, when elected in 1997, claimed to represent a "new" form of politics and a new way of running the country. Tony Blair sought to create a country with equal opportunities for all. It would be based on "meritocracy" – those with talent and an ethos of hard work should succeed.

Those who opposed change and "modernisation", the so-called "forces of conservatism", be it trade unions at one end of the class system, or rich elites at the other, would be swept aside. There was to be a "new" Britain with no favours for vested interests or for those with contacts. New Labour would end "Tory sleaze" and "jobs for the boys". New Labour, as Tony Blair famously said, would be "whiter than white".

> The Wakeham report was a disappointment, even to Lord Wakeham himself.

Such a project would surely mean the end for the Lords, the "best club in Britain". It was even argued that the current status of the Lords violates Article 3 of Protocol 1 to the European Convention of Human Rights (ECHR), of which Britain is a signatory. This commits states "to undertake to hold free elections…which will ensure the free expression of the opinion of the people in the choice of the legislature".

Surely, an elected Lords, perhaps by some form of proportional representation, could re-energise democracy by creating new, younger and more representative decision makers?

Labour completed the first stage of its Lords reform in 1999 when all but 92 of the 750 hereditary peers lost their right to sit and vote in the Lords. However, Labour was unable to agree a method of "pensioning off" these remaining hereditary peers. Labour's reforming credentials were damaged in the rows over Prime Minister Tony Blair's strategy of unprecedented numbers of new Labour life peers. New peers included Melvyn Bragg, the arts broadcaster, the murder mystery writer, Ruth Rendell and supermarket head, David Sainsbury, a strong supporter of New Labour and contributor to party funds.

Tony Blair stated, however, that the massive increase in the number of Labour peers was justified in balancing out the historic Conservative dominance in the Upper House. The phrase, "Tony's cronies", entered the political vocabulary. This ultimately led to an investigation by the Metropolitan Police, the so-called "Cash for Honours" enquiry.

The Wakeham Report

A Royal Commission, headed by Lord Wakeham was set up to examine the future, if any, of the Lords. "A House for the Future", was published in January 2000.

The report was a disappointment, even to Lord Wakeham himself. Most critics have felt its reforms didn't go far enough. While it did recognise a need for greater regional representation, for broadly equal numbers of men and women and for a better reflection of the country's ethnic mix, it proposed to leave untouched the current balance of power between the Commons and the new upper house. It also fudged the question of what the new upper house should be called.

Wakeham's key proposals were:
- A new chamber should be set up which should have a total of around 550 members. Of these, a "significant minority" should be elected members. The exact number was not specified.
- "Appointed Members" were to be chosen by an Independent Appointments Commission. Members would serve a fixed term of 15 years, renewable for another 15 years.
- At least 30 per cent of the appointed members should be women. Ethnic minority groups should be represented in proportion to the population as a whole.

Activities

- What are the main criticisms of the House of Lords?
- Why do some people support the existence of the House of Lords?
- What were the main criticisms of the Wakeham report?

Powers of the House of Lords

Under the Parliament Acts of 1911 and 1949, the Lords has the right to delay bills for up to one year, but it has no right at all to interfere with finance bills. The Parliament Acts have only been used twice in recent years to push through legislation against the will of the Lords: to pass the War Crimes Bill of 1991 and to amend the law on the age of consent for gay men in 1999.

Since 1945, the Lords has not taken a vote on the second reading of any bill promised in the Government's election manifesto or (more recently) in the government's legislative programme for the session. The second reading is the stage at which legislation is discussed in principle, before being considered in greater detail at third reading.

The House of Lords and anti-terrorism legislation

By February 2007, the Lords had defeated the Blair Governments more than 350 times. There have been several high profile clashes between the Commons and the Lords.

Former Home Secretary David Blunkett's anti-terrorist legislation was comprehensively mauled by the Lords. The bill, drafted in the wake of the terrorist attacks on the USA in September 2001, contained several highly controversial new powers, such as the right to detain foreigners suspected of terrorism without trial.

After ten separate defeats in the House of Lords, David Blunkett was forced to make an important concession. One key clause - banning the incitement of religious hatred - was removed from the bill, after being thrown out twice by the Lords. But detention without trial and several other controversial powers stayed in - and have since become law.

The House of Lords and fox hunting

The House of Commons passed legislation to ban hunting by a huge majority (more than 200 MPs) in January 2001. But, just before the June 2001 General Election, the bill was blocked in the Lords. Time ran out, and the fox hunting bill was one of a number which the government scrapped, as it cleared the legislative decks for the General Election. The Fox Hunting Act was eventually passed in 2004. Fox hunting, in England and Wales, remains legal but it is now illegal to kill foxes with hounds.

The House of Lords and the age of consent

Led by the late Tory Peer Lady Young, the Lords fought tooth and nail not to lower the age of consent for gay men from 18 to 16. The Lords voted the House of Commons bill down twice (in July 1998 and April 1999), before the Government used the Parliament Acts to force the bill through in November 2000. In all, the process took nearly three years.

The future of the House of Lords

In March 2007, the House of Commons voted by a majority of 113 MPs for a fully elected House of Lords. But peers rejected this and backed an all-appointed second chamber! However, the days of non-elected peers in the Lords appear, this time, to be numbered. The big question is when, rather than if.

A cross party group on Lords reform has been formed, led by Leader of the House of Commons, Jack Straw. It faces many hurdles. Both life and appointed peers are likely to resist their elimination. The cross-party group needs to be clear on what powers an elected Lords should have. They need to decide an electoral system for Lords elections, and how long Lords may serve in office.

Activities

- What reforms has Labour made to the House of Lords?
- Describe key interventions by the House of Lords in the passage of government bills.
- Why might the House of Lords be around for some time yet?

Chapter 5: Power and Influence on Government

The strength of the Government's majority in the House of Commons and the state of the opposition are big factors in the influence of pressure groups. For the majority of his time as Prime Minister, Tony Blair's Government had large Commons majorities. At the same time, the Conservative Opposition was divided and in poor fettle. Both Government and individual Labour MPs were therefore not as vulnerable to attention from pressure groups.

Outsider and Insider Pressure groups

The Stop the War coalition could be categorised as being an "outsider group" in terms of its relationship with the Labour Government.

Pressure groups are usually categorised as having either "Outsider" or "Insider" status. An Insider group is one which plays a fundamental part in the governance of the country. Government will consult with the group. There will be regular meetings and correspondence between pressure group and Government. The pressure group will have an impact on Government policy.

On the other hand, Outsider groups are on the margins of decision making. Government will disagree with their aims. As such, the Outsider group adopts different methods to bring its cause to the attention of the public and Government. Outsider groups will rely more on media friendly attention seeking activities than the low key activities favoured by those on the inside track of decision making.

Outsider pressure groups

Not all outsider groups are the same. There are degrees of being an outsider group. It is fair to say that a terrorist group such as al-Qaeda is right on the margins. Way out! The Stop the War coalition, whilst a perfectly legal and legitimate pressure group, is on the outer track too.

But, outsider pressure groups which have democratic aims and start on the outside can move inside and be successful. The campaign against the deportation of the Vucaj family is a case in point.

The Vucaj family, who had lived in Glasgow for some years, failed in their application for asylum after a long drawn out process. In this time, the children had grown up in Scotland and attended, very successfully, Drumchapel High School. A campaign, focused on the Scottish Parliament, raised public awareness. While the campaign did not succeed in overturning the ruling against the Vucaj family, and they had to return to Albania, the Scottish Parliament is now in discussions with Westminster about how it can prevent so-called "dawn raids" on unsuccessful asylum seekers. The Glasgow Girls won the Scottish Campaign of the Year Award in 2005 at the annual Scottish Politician of the Year ceremony.

Insider pressure groups

Pressure groups which have expert knowledge of an issue and whose aims are compatible with the political persuasion of the Government of the day are more likely to find themselves with "insider" status.

The Prime Minister will seek out the views of leading business people. If the CBI says that it does not want taxes to rise, Gordon Brown, and his Chancellor of the Exchequer, will listen carefully.

The British Medical Association which represents the country's doctors, are also on the "inside track" of Government. Such pressure groups have a lot of expertise and public support. Government Ministers, traditionally, are keen to seek out their views and have them "on side". For example, if the Government

Lobbying

Pressure groups need to be strategic about who they seek to apply pressure to. There is little point in "lobbying" Westminster, if it is a devolved, or local issue, the group is concerned about. Increasingly, the Scottish Parliament is the focus for pressure group lobbying, as the groups realise the issue in question is a devolved one, rather than a reserved issue, which is the responsibility of Westminster.

The Scottish Parliament has strict rules on lobbying. As part of the Code of Conduct for members of the Scottish Parliament, MSPs must declare any interest they have in organisations or payments/gifts they have received from organisations.

Theyworkforyou.com is a website which tries to make it easier for the public to see how their representatives are voting and easier for the public to put pressure on them.

Lobbying takes its name from the 'lobbies' or hallways of Parliament where MPs and peers gather before and after debates in the Commons and Lords chambers.

In the past, those who sought to influence the opinions of MPs or peers physically gathered at the 'lobbies', seeking to persuade members of the merits of their particular viewpoint. MPs are still 'lobbied' directly by their constituents, local businesses and campaign groups on many issues

Nowadays, the term lobbying often refers more specifically to the work of private companies, known as 'lobbyists', which are employed by organisations to represent their views to Parliament in a variety of

ways - by arranging meetings, organising protests or providing briefing material. Lobbyists will sometimes claim to have special access to Ministers or be on particularly good relations with Ministers in order to win business. Lobbying, or public affairs as it is usually known as, is now a multi-million pound industry.

The Hansard Society estimates that MPs can be lobbied by professional public affairs companies as often as 100 times per week. Lobbying has been criticised as unethical, as not everyone can afford the fees charged by public affairs agencies. It is argued that those with wealth should not be able to buy influence those without wealth cannot. There are strict rules over the relationships Ministers can have with lobbyists, and public affairs companies must observe a code of conduct.

Early in Tony Blair's premiership The Observer newspaper revealed how lobbyists close to the Prime Minister's inner circle were offering their clients meetings at No. 10 and insider information. The scandal, which led to a high profile lobbyist, Derek Draper, resigning from his job with the public relations company, GPC Market Access, became known as "Lobbygate". New Labour, which had campaigned against "Tory sleaze", had committed itself to being whiter than white.

In 1999, Lobbygate came to Scotland. The Scottish Parliament sets high standards for itself in openness and accountability in its decision-making. However, The Observer alleged that an undercover journalist had evidence that a public affairs company, Beattie Media, had executives who were offering preferential access to Scottish ministers. The company boasted that Jack McConnell was a former employee of the firm. A parliamentary probe by the Scottish Parliament's Standards committee cleared Jack McConnell of any wrongdoing.

In addition to "open" lobbying, the United Kingdom political parties have been accused of trying to raise campaign funds by offering peerages and other honors. Since peers sit in the House of Lords, they are in a position to amend Bills on their way to becoming Acts of Parliament - a very influential position. The rules of Parliament do, however, require participants in debates to 'declare their interest'. The 'sale' of peerages is a criminal offence. To circumvent this law, it is alleged that some contributions are given not as outright gifts, but as loans.

Activities

- Describe how lobbyists can influence government decisions.
- Why have public affairs firms been criticised?
- Explain why "Lobbygate" was a problem for the Blair government.

Cash for honours?

The Blair government landed itself in trouble when it was alleged to have given peerages in the House of Lords to those who lent money to the Labour Party. In 2006 it emerged that, to fund their 2005 General Election campaign, Labour was secretly loaned nearly £14m and the Conservatives £16m. The Liberal Democrats said they borrowed £850,000 from three backers. Labour's lenders included Sir David Garrard, a property developer, who lent the party £2.3m, Lord David Sainsbury of the supermarket chain who lent £2m, and Richard Caring, owner of the upmarket Ivy restaurant in London. It was alleged by SNP MP, Angus MacNeil, that Labour had offered donors peerages in return for the loans.

Labour's chief fundraiser, Lord Levy, nicknamed "Lord Cashpoint", was the man most deeply implicated. Tony Blair was questioned by police, the first PM in history ever to be questioned. The Cash for Honours investigation by Scotland Yard concluded in July 2007. It found that the Government had not broken any rules over awarding honours.

Four people were arrested during the inquiries, which cost the taxpayer over £1 million. They were Lord Levy, Tony Blair's former chief fundraiser, Sir Christopher Evans, a prominent businessman and donor to the Labour Party, Des Smith, a former head teacher involved with Labour's City Academy Programme, and Ruth Turner, Mr Blair's former director of government relations. All insisted all along that they were innocent. While the verdict was a triumph for Tony Blair, the process has called for tighter rules over party fund raising.

Gordon Brown and the New Politics

It is early days to assess the Brown Premiership, but early indications are that Gordon Brown wants to make his mark as a different Prime Minister from Tony Blair.

This is partly self-interest. Brown needs to show that he is different from Blair and will take the country in a new direction. He promises to restore cabinet decision making and strengthen cabinet committees. Gordon Brown held two cabinet meetings in his first two days as Prime Minister. The second meeting lasted almost two hours. Tony Blair's Cabinet meetings, when he held them, sometimes lasted fifteen minutes. Gordon Brown has stated that he wants to restore civil servants to positions of influence, rather than have as many special advisers briefing ministers. He is also considering granting the House of Commons the power to decide on war.

The problem for any Opposition is that if they come up with sensible solutions, the Government just steals them!

Former Liberal Democrat leader Lord Ashdown was invited to join Gordon Brown's "government of all the talents".

Gordon Brown has reached out beyond the Labour Party for members of his Cabinet. In his quest for a "government of all the talents", he has invited former Liberal Democrat leader Lord Paddy Ashdown, former CBI chief Sir Digby Jones and former UN boss Sir Mark Malloch (Malloch is now the new Minister for Africa, Asia and the UN). Gordon Brown has also recruited television's Apprentice star and business tycoon Sir Alan Sugar to his new Business Leaders' Council, which will provide business advice and feedback to Downing Street. Gordon Brown has appealed to One Nation Conservatives to join Labour in order to "shape and enlarge the middle ground". While Gordon Brown may have a different style of leadership from Tony Blair, his political direction is very similar. In September 2007 he famously invited former Conservative Prime Minister Margaret Thatcher to Downing Street for talks. He praised her as a "conviction politician".

Gordon Brown is very keen to re establish values of "Britishness" in the UK's political culture. As part of his attempt to define what Britishness actually means, the Prime Minister has suggested that Britain should have a written constitution that would enshrine the rights of the individual and spell out exactly the nation's political procedures.

A constitutional review

This is part of Gordon Brown's wider agenda to reform parliament, solving amongst other things, disputes over Prime Ministerial power and the West Lothian question. Unlike many other countries, the UK does not have a single, written constitution. Instead, the UK is governed by a series of protocols and informal customs which exist in a diverse set of books, documents and law reports. It is argued that the time has come to update these rules, some of which go back to the signing of Magna Carta by King John in 1215. For example, it is UK protocol that the Prime Minister alone has the right to decide the date of a General Election. The debacle of the November 2007 General Election (that never was) has led to many calls for the UK to have fixed parliamentary terms.

Declining public trust in politics and politicians, low election turnouts, disaffection towards the UK by a minority of British born Muslims and the election of an SNP Government in Scotland have all led Gordon Brown to question how the British state can survive in the 21st century.

It is ironic that it is the Prime Minister who is considering modernisation of the UK constitution:

for it was his mishandling of the decision whether or not to hold a General election in November 2007 which made him lose face so badly.

A Conservative Government would ban MPs from Scottish constituencies from voting on non-devolved issues. This, it is feared, will only add to calls for a break up of the UK, rather than end the arguments. Sun columnist, Kelvin McKenzie, blasted on BBC Radio 5 Live that "the Scots live solely on the handouts of the clever English generating wealth in London and the south east."

McKenzie may hold extreme views, but he does articulate a resentment some English voters feel about the constitutional difficulty of a Prime Minister, who represents a Scottish constituency, running England, while English MPs have no say over many matters which are now devolved to Scotland.

> "The Scots live solely on the handouts of the clever English generating wealth in London and the south east"
> Kelvin McKenzie

Activities

- Explain what is meant by Cash for Honours?
- What does Gordon Brown mean by a "Government of all the talents"?
- Why does Gordon Brown seek to promote his "British" credentials?
- Why is Gordon Brown keen to "modernise" the UK constitution?

The Big Picture

When we speak of "ideologies" and political parties, we refer to ideas and beliefs which bind members of that party together. These are ideas which lead to political parties being formed and which motivate people to enter politics by joining parties whose ideas they share. While, in theory, each political party should have a distinct ideology of its own (a "unique selling point" or USP), in the modern day, ideologies cut across UK political parties.

There are some Labour MPs who may feel more at ease with Liberal Democrat ideas. There may be Conservative MPs who agree with much of New Labour. Within parties, there are different ideologies too. For example, David Cameron's supporters within the Conservative Party believe in many different values from "traditionalist" Conservatives within the party.

Many political analysts today speak of a lack of ideology in modern British politics. In the 1980s, the Labour Party moved to the Left and was closely associated with socialist ideologies. By contrast, the Conservatives under Margaret Thatcher moved to the Right, supporting more libertarian views. The growing space in the political centre ground was filled by a new party, the Social Democratic Party, which later merged with the Liberal Party, to form the Liberal Democrats.

Tony Blair's New Labour changed this political landscape. Blair moved Labour all the way from the Left, across to the Right. New Labour's dominance since 1997 has forced the other political parties to review their ideologies and their USP.

The USPs of the main UK parties are:
* New Labour   Social justice
* The Conservatives   Individualism
* Liberal Democrats   Liberalism
* Scottish National Party Scottish nationalism

It is therefore wrong to say that there is *no* ideology in UK politics. It is more accurate to say that there is now a lack of real ideological difference between the main UK political parties. The parties' ideologies have converged around the centre ground of political values. This is where the parties believe the ideologies of the voters are.

While the parties put their own unique "spin" on their beliefs, the dominant ideology today is that of social democracy. The leaderships of the UK parties agree on supporting enterprise and private ownership. Yet, they agree on the importance of high quality public services. The parties agree that the role of government is not to run the economy, but to provide an economic environment where both private and public services can thrive. They agree on the importance of low taxation and that public spending must be "prudent". They accept that there is a link between poverty and low educational achievement and crime. They accept that government must provide support to those in need. But this support should be based on "a hand up, not a hand out".

So, across a whole range of social and economic policies there is broad agreement. The parties however differ by degree. They also differ on specific policies, messages and vocabulary. They each have a distinct "core" vote, while at the same time they each target the "floating voters" required to win elections.

Each of the UK parties has a Scottish version. To varying degrees, the Scottish versions have the freedom to devise their own ideology and policies.

In Scotland, the SNP, a comparatively young political party, has matured and has moved away from a "catch all" party of protest towards a party of government which has a clear social democratic ideology. Each of the UK parties has a Scottish version. To varying degrees, the Scottish versions have the freedom to devise their own ideology and policies. While the Scottish parties' ideological approach remains faithful to the UK parent, Scottish political parties tend to emphasise a greater role for the public sector than their UK party does.

Within parties, there is a great deal of competition and rivalry. As one experienced MP famously said to a newly elected MP, "your opponents sit over there, the enemy sits behind you". All UK parties have their different inner party pressure groupings with their own ideological, sometimes personal, agendas.

tradition, hence Tony Blair and Gordon Brown's "big tent" approach represents continuity as well as change in the party's ideology.

In September 2007, Prime Minister Gordon Brown invited former Conservative leader and Prime Minister, Margaret Thatcher to 10 Downing Street for tea. Gordon Brown praised Margaret Thatcher as "a conviction politician". Many Labour supporters were aghast. Margaret Thatcher's ideas and policies were everything Labour opposed. Margaret Thatcher personally may have been the reason why many Labour activists entered politics! Yet, here was Gordon Brown, a Labour Prime Minister singing her praises.

It is all part of Gordon Brown's, and his predecessor, Tony Blair's idea of "the big tent". The big tent approach means that Labour should have policies and presentation which attract voters across the political spectrum, from Left to Right. This means that rival parties

Former Conservative leader Margaret Thatcher. Prime Minister Gordon Brown praised her as "a conviction politician".

struggle to form an identity and appeal which could challenge Labour. The Conservatives either have to copy Labour, or move to the Right. This may please some Conservative activists, but almost certainly will mean electoral defeat. Likewise, the Liberal Democrats have a similar choice of occupying the same "centre ground" as Labour, or of moving to the Left.

Tensions between the inner party groups grow with electoral defeat. Parties exist to win power. When power isn't won, there is reflection as to whether the direction pursued was the correct one or whether another direction is required. But, voters do not like parties which are not united. Too much introspection and feuding can lead to demoralisation and defeat. A vicious circle!

Chapter 6   Party Ideologies

New Labour's Big Tent

Since its formation in 1900, the Labour Party has always been a coalition of differing ideologies. The phrase, "a broad church" of opinions, is used to describe the different strands of opinion found in the Labour Party; from Marxist to social democratic to socially conservative. The creation of "New Labour" in 1994 in some respects makes a break with Labour's traditions. But, there is no one "true" Labour

Labour's big tent approach means the party will draw up manifesto commitments containing policies which will appeal to "traditional" Labour supporters, but also to voters whose instincts are towards the Conservative Party. The National Minimum Wage and spending on the NHS are policies which keep voters on the Left relatively content. However, more "right wing" policies, such as cuts in income tax and support for immigration controls, appeal to more conservative voters.

Tony Blair was widely seen as a "big tent" politician, pulling in the votes of traditional Conservative voters. Gordon Brown, with his Scottish and trade union background, may feel he has to make a public gesture of his support for traditionally Conservative policies. This explains his date with Baroness Thatcher.

It also explains why Gordon Brown uses cleverly worded phrases, such as "British jobs for British workers". Gordon Brown used this phrase at the 2007 Labour Party conference in response to appeals from trade unions to protect British workers from companies "outsourcing" work to foreign factories where labour is cheaper. However, his use of the words, "British jobs for British workers" was deliberate. By inserting the word "British" twice, against a blue conference backdrop instead of the traditional Labour red, Brown was appealing to right wing voters who believe immigrants are taking jobs which should be there for British workers.

Activities

- Why do political parties have a Unique Selling Point (USP)?
- What is meant by the phrase "a broad church"?
- Why does Gordon Brown's "big tent" approach explain his meeting with former Conservative leader Margaret Thatcher?

Old and New Labour

The phrase "New Labour" is not used so much by the Labour Party now. It is very much associated with former leader Tony Blair. While Blair was the most successful Labour leader ever, measured in terms of electoral wins, he ended his term as Premier in the shadow of the war in Iraq and the Cash for Honours scandal.

Blair was exonerated of misleading the House of Commons over the existence of weapons of mass destruction in Iraq. Likewise, the Metropolitan Police's enquiry into alleged Cash for Honours found no charge to make against the former Prime Minister. Yet, Gordon Brown feels he has to "move on" and establish his own identity as Prime Minister. The term "New Labour" may not be so widely used, but New Labour is very much what Gordon Brown will govern as.

In what ways is "New Labour" different from "Old Labour"?

Supporters of "old Labour" would see the achievements of the 1945-51 Labour Government as the party's golden period. They may even be nostalgic about Harold Wilson and Jim Callaghan's governments in the 1960s and 1970s.

The Labour Government of 1945 introduced the National Health Service and the welfare state. It brought many private industries into public ownership. It sought to redistribute wealth from the rich to the poor. Despite winning more votes in the 1951 General Election than the Conservatives, Labour lost the 1951 election to the Conservatives.

Tony Blair saw the creation of "New Labour" as essential if the Labour Party was to win power again.

Prior to Tony Blair, the Labour Party had only been in power for 21 of its first ninety-seven years of existence. By the mid 1990s, Labour had lost three elections in a row and had been out of office for eighteen years. Moves had been made by successive leaders, such as Neil Kinnock and John Smith, to "moderate" the party's policies and image. However, upon election as leader in 1994, Tony Blair felt a decisive re-branding and "modernisation" of the Labour Party was essential if Labour was ever to win power again.

New Labour The Brand

On taking over as Labour leader, Tony Blair set about abolishing Clause 4 of the party's constitution. Clause 4 was an obscure paragraph in Labour's constitution which, sort of, committed Labour to public ownership. Inscribed on each party member's membership card, Clause 4 read; 'To secure for the producers by hand or by brain the full fruits of their industry, and the most equitable distribution thereof that may be possible, upon the basis of the common ownership of the means of production and the best obtainable system of popular administration and control of each industry and service.'

Most voters would not have heard of Clause 4 and cared even less. When Blair proposed to replace it with something else, something "more modern", Labour activists were suspicious. Why go to all the bother of replacing something few people even know about? This was precisely Blair's point. He wanted voters to talk about this new constitution. For Blair it was a symbolic re-launch of the Labour Party.

Armed with a new Constitution and the ritual defeat of the Left in the party, he could talk to the country about "New Labour". Labour's new Clause 4 part 2(a) now reads; "we work for

"a dynamic economy, serving the public interest, in which the enterprise of the market and the rigour of competition are joined with the forces of partnership and co-operation to produce the wealth the nation needs and the opportunity for all to work and prosper with a thriving private sector and high-quality public services where those undertakings essential to the common good are either owned by the public or accountable to them"

Quite a difference. Words such as "enterprise", "competition", "thriving private sector" are in. Words such as "equitable" and "common ownership" are out.

"Tough on crime, tough on the causes of crime" was a classic Blair Third way soundbite.

Activities

- Explain why the phrase, "British jobs for British workers", is a Big Tent sound bite.
- In what ways is "New Labour" different from "Old Labour"?
- Why was Tony Blair so keen to change Clause 4 of the party's constitution?
- In what ways is the new Labour Party constitution different from the old one?

New Labour and the Third Way

Blair's mantra was that Labour had to abandon "old" ways of thinking. The party had to review all its policies with a fresh sheet of paper. The party had to forget ideologies of socialism and concentrate on "what works". This non-ideology was an ideology! It was the "third way". Old Labour's collectivist and "tax and spend" approach was seen as the first way. The Thatcherite individualist approach was seen as the second. The third way would support the rights of the individual to become wealthy, but

the state would seek to support people to become independent.

It was accompanied by many Americanisms. Both Blair and Brown were big admirers of President Clinton's successful campaign in promoting the brand of "New Democrats". New Labour adopted much of Clinton's vocabulary. The welfare state would no longer offer "hand outs, but a hand up". The state would help those out of work get back to work via "New Deals". Many social security benefits were replaced with complex "tax credits" whose claimants often had to be at work in order to have any kind of eligibility.

Perhaps the classic Third Way statement was Tony Blair's classic claim that New Labour would be "tough on crime and tough on the causes of crime". Among the key group of voters in marginal constituencies, Old Labour had a reputation for being "soft" on criminals and their anti-social behaviour. Labour appeared to make excuses for criminality, blaming poverty and family breakdown, rather than protect hard-working, law-abiding citizens.

Focus group discussions and electoral research targeted floating voters in the C1/C2 social classes as the key electoral group New Labour had to reach.

Sometimes described as "Mondeo Man", Labour had to prove that it would be tough on criminals. However, at the same time, to reassure traditional Labour supporters, New Labour promised to put in place policies which would tackle the causes of criminality, such as long-term unemployment. With this Third Way approach, New Labour could pull in voters who had left the party in the 1980s for the Conservatives, yet keep the support of its "core" vote.

Activities

- Explain what you understand by the third way.
- In what ways has New Labour been influenced by American politics?
- Why was Labour's new approach to crime classic third way?

Scottish Conservative leader Annabel Goldie is a "One Nation" Conservative.

The Conservatives in Opposition

The Conservative Party, officially called The Conservative and Unionist Party, is the UK's biggest and most successful political party. The Conservative Party is descended from the Tory Party of the eighteenth and nineteenth centuries. Its members are still commonly referred to as Tories and the party is still often referred to as the Tory Party.

While Conservative membership numbers have fallen in recent years, something all the UK parties have in common, the party still has more members (about 290,000) than Labour and the Liberal Democrats combined (around 200,000 and 70,000 respectively). The Conservatives were in power in the House of Commons for 2/3 of the 20th century. The Conservatives can also claim to be the only party to have achieved over 50% of the vote in Scotland.

The Conservative Party has always boated of its lack of ideology. Its supporters have ridiculed themselves as "the stupid party" as, by comparison with Labour, Conservative members are less inclined to involve themselves in ideological debate. The Conservatives, by definition, believe in conserving society's values. Social change, if it has to come, should be gradual. Whereas Labour activists are, or were, forever lobbying their leaders to become more ideological, Conservative activists have, traditionally, been more deferential towards their leaders.

Conservatives value pragmatism more than ideology. So long as the party was winning elections, as it mostly was, there was little demand for ideological revolutions in social or economic policy.

Up until the rise of "the New Right" in the 1980s in both the UK and the USA, the dominant ideology of the Conservative Party was "One Nation Conservatism". The term derives from Benjamin Disraeli's political novel, *The Two Nations*, in which he described Britain as "Two nations between whom there is no intercourse and no sympathy; who are as ignorant of each other's habits, thoughts, and feelings, as if they were dwellers in different zones, or inhabitants of different planets: the rich and the poor."

There are still One Nation Conservatives around. Big hitters such as Kenneth Clarke and Malcolm Rifkind ally themselves with this tradition. The Tory Reform group is the inner party pressure group which champions One Nation Conservative values. One Nation Conservatives, while strong supporters of free enterprise, believe that the wealthy should make a financial and social contribution to the society. They believe in the welfare state and the need to minimise the impact of inequalities in society. They are not socialists. One Nation Conservatives believe in equality of opportunity, not equality. Conservative Prime Ministers such as Harold McMillan and Edward Heath were One Nation Conservatives.

The Challenge of the Libertarians

Prime Minister Edward Heath's humiliation at the hands of the trade unions in the 1970s gave support to a competing Conservative ideology; free market liberalism. Today's Conservative libertarians support the "No Turning Back" and "Conservative Way Forward" party pressure groups. Influenced by the writings of economist Milton Friedman, the neo-liberals gathered around new Conservative leader Margaret Thatcher, who favoured individual solutions, rather than the One Nation Conservative's collective solutions.

Margaret Thatcher routed the One Nation Conservatives. The "post war consensus" between the leaders of Labour and Conservative Parties were torn up. The Libertarians believed the welfare state had created a "dependency culture". For them, the welfare state made people lazy and lacking in independence. They believed that One Nation Conservatives had been complicit in building a "nanny state" which took responsibility away from individuals to look after themselves.

The solution was, as leading libertarian Norman Tebbit put it, to "get the state off people's backs". Following election victories in 1979, 1983 and 1987, the Conservatives followed a libertarian agenda. Industries were privatised. Taxes were cut. Benefits were cut. Competition was introduced to public services such as health and education. Laws were passed which restricted the rights of trade unions. Inequalities in British society grew. One Nation Conservatives despaired. But libertarians believed that inequality wasn't all bad. "Hard-working families" should not be taxed by Government to fund benefits for those unwilling to take responsibility.

For the libertarians, inequality was actually necessary to reward success and motivate the less successful to become more independent. Margaret Thatcher's demise in 1990 damaged the libertarian cause. Since the 1990s, and especially since the rise of New Labour (which, arguably, embraced many of the ideas of the libertarians), the Conservatives have yet to resolve the ideological direction the party should pursue.

John Major was a pragmatist rather than an ideologue. His successor, William Hague, sought to put "clear blue water" between the Conservatives

Former Conservative leader Michael Howard was a libertarian by instinct. But, he recognised the need to bring the Conservatives back into the political mainstream.

and Labour. His rightward move, supported by the libertarians, was spectacularly unsuccessful. Kenneth Clarke, standard bearer of the One Nation Conservatives, once again stood and failed to be elected Conservative leader. Hague's successor, Iain Duncan Smith, came from a libertarian background. His failure to establish a successful USP for the Conservatives (ironically Iain Duncan Smith has risen again within the party as a leading One Nation Conservative) brought another libertarian assault on New Labour by Michael Howard.

While very much a Thatcher admirer, Howard faced the prospect of being marginalised by the Liberal Democrats. To the disappointment of the libertarians, Howard moderated his libertarian instincts and brought the Conservative back into the political centre.

The 2005 General Election was in many ways a disaster for the Conservatives. The party bottomed out at 33% of the national vote. But, it clawed back 33 seats, while Labour lost 47. Any credible Conservative leader had to bring the party into the centre ground of politics. He/she also had to carve out a new identity for the Conservatives. The "Greed is good" days of the 1980s no longer appealed to voters who worried about wider societal breakdown. Perhaps the long term success of the libertarians lies in the fact that the UK political centre is now much further to the right than when Margaret Thatcher took power. Tony Blair, and now Gordon Brown, have accepted many of Margaret Thatcher's values which were so contested by Labour back in the 1980s.

Traditionalist Conservatives

The Conservatives traditionally support "family values". The Church of England until recently had the reputation, deserved or otherwise, as "the Conservative Party at prayer". Traditionalist Conservatives oppose relaxations on laws over homosexuality, immigration, and are fundamentally opposed to the European Union.

Traditionalist Conservatives have been shocked, almost on a daily basis, by David Cameron's leadership. Cameron's more liberal approach to family values and social breakdown strikes at the core of many values of traditionalist Conservatism. The Cornerstone Group (Faith, Flag and Family) are the leading advocates of Traditionalist Conservatism. Gay Conservative MP Alan Duncan once referred to the Cornerstone Group as the party's "Taleban tendency".

Activities

- In what ways are Labour Party activists different from Conservative Party activists?
- Explain what is meant by "One Nation" Conservatism.
- In what ways is libertarian conservatism different from One Nation Conservatism
- Why might it be said that the libertarians have been successful in the long term?

Cameron's Conservatives

In 2005, after yet another election defeat, the Conservatives were forced to re-examine their ideology and direction. The usual suspects stood for the leadership. One Nation supporter Kenneth Clarke threw his hat in the ring for the third time. Liam Fox and David Davis, who had agendas which appealed to both libertarian and traditionalist Conservatives also stood. But, this time the Conservatives wanted a different appeal. David Cameron offered a "new" approach. Rather than competing against Labour on Traditional or Left or Right Conservatism, Cameron offered a "quality of

life" agenda.

Party Chairman, Theresa May, famously said that the Conservatives had become known as the "nasty party". While British society had "moved on" from the values of the 1980s, the Conservatives had become associated with intolerance, selfishness and xenophobia. Former Party Chairman, Brian Mawhinney, observed that the party had "created the impression that if you weren't in a traditional nuclear family, then we weren't interested in you". Cameron offered to place the Conservatives back into the centre ground.

David Cameron has worked hard to change the Conservatives' image as "the nasty party".

Describing himself as "a modern, compassionate Conservative", Cameron promised to broaden the party's appeal and modernise the party's image. His stated aim was to "make people feel good about being a Conservative again". Some Conservatives believe Cameron's approach is the answer. As one commentator put it, "after the baldheads and retreads that have preceded him in the post, Cameron is exciting". Others, from different ideological approaches, believe that the party needs to stick to its "core values" and not become a Conservative version of New Labour.

Norman Tebbit has likened Cameron to Pol Pot, "intent on purging even the memory of Thatcherism before building a New Modern Compassionate Green Globally Aware Party". In July 2007, while Cameron was on a fact-finding mission to Africa, it was reported in the press that at least two, and as many as six, Conservative MPs had sent letters to the chair of the Conservative 1922 Committee demanding a no confidence vote in Mr Cameron's leadership. Having spent his first 18 months as leader repositioning the party in the Centre, he finds himself under attack from Left and Right.

David Cameron saved himself, and the Conservative Party's chances of electoral defeat from a "snap" General Election, with a barnstorming speech at the 2007 Conservative Party conference. Speaking without notes or an autocue, Cameron successfully projected the Conservatives as a credible party of government. His Shadow Chancellor, George Osborne, unveiled a new tax policy; a Conservative government would raise the threshold at which people paid Inheritance Tax from £250,000 to £1 million. This would be paid for by a new tax on non-domiciles, the growing number of über rich who pay little or no tax because, legally, they do not live in the UK.

This was classic Blair and classic big tent politics. Those on the Right, core Conservative voters, were galvanised because they would pay less Inheritance Tax. Voters in marginal seats were pleased that "non-doms", such as Chelsea FC owner Ramon Abramovich, would now make more of a financial contribution to society. Within a week, Chancellor Alasdair Darling raised the threshold at which Inheritance Tax is paid to £600,000.

Activities

- Why was the Conservative Party described as "the nasty party"?
- Why has David Cameron's leadership been controversial to traditionalist Conservatives?
- Why could it be said that David Cameron is now practicing big tent politics?

The Liberal Democrats and the Centre Ground

The modern Liberal Democrats are the product of a merger in 1988 between the Liberal Party and the Social Democratic Party. The Liberal Party was once the leading party in British politics, but declined after the formation of the Labour Party and universal suffrage. There has not been a Liberal Prime Minister since David Lloyd George in 1922.

The Social Democratic Party (SDP) was formed in 1981 by a group of right wing Labour MPs who became unhappy at the party's move to the Left. Realising that there was no future for two parties of the political centre, the Liberals and SDP first formed the Alliance, then fully merged the two parties together.

There were tensions. The Liberal Party was more socially liberal than the SDP. Many Liberal activists were members of liberal pressure groups such as the Campaign for Nuclear Disarmament (CND) which the SDP completely opposed. Nevertheless, the Liberal Democrats, often referred to as the Lib Dems, under the leadership of Paddy Ashdown gradually became the third force in UK politics. In 2005, leader Charles Kennedy set the party the target of replacing the Conservatives as the main opposition party to Labour.

The key issue facing the Liberal Democrats today is where to place themselves in the political market place. Labour has placed a "big tent", from left to right, across the political spectrum. David Cameron has acknowledged the errors of his predecessors in being outside the big tent to the right. He has moved the Conservatives into the centre, and at times, with his promises to reduce wealth inequality, to the left of Labour.

In a sense these should be the best years for the Liberal Democrats. The party that has always claimed to be free of class war and vested interests finds itself in a political climate where all the major parties

> The key issue facing the Liberal Democrats today is where to place themselves in the political market place... The Liberal Democrats' problem is that the policies which make them unique are the ones that Labour and the Conservatives won't touch.

accept that the old politics is dying out. There are still many parts of the country where it is unthinkable for voters to leave their traditional class-based parties behind. But, as the economy that created class politics is being transformed, a new, middle-ground politics, which emphasises the policies the Liberal Democrats have been supporting for years is being constructed too.

So, in this crowded political space, how can the Liberal Democrats differentiate themselves? What can their unique selling point (USP) be? The Liberal Democrats' problem is that the policies which make them unique are the ones that Labour and the Conservatives won't touch. Tax increases for the rich. Putting green taxes on flying and high carbon emitting cars. Tough penalties for those who won't recycle. Many voters agree that these are well meaning policies and may in fact be highly sensible. But, there tends to be a difference between what voters in opinion polls say they want and what they do in the privacy of the polling booth. Everyone wants to save the planet. Most people feel that the super rich earn too much. Everyone knows that we need to recycle more.

But, most voters do not vote for governments which promise tax increases. They do not like being punished for going on holiday or for getting a nice car. If the Liberal Democrats come up with a good policy, Labour and Conservatives tend to steal it. The Liberal Democrats have that classic dilemma which faces a centre party. Should it continue to market itself as a party to the left of Labour or should it try to re connect with voters in the Conservative held seats that represent its best chance of electoral gain?

If the UK had a proportional voting system the Liberal Democrats would have a greater chance of power. But, in the increasingly Presidential style election campaigns we have, in a First Past the Post contest, many voters are forced into an either/or position. The accepted wisdom is that overall the Liberal Democrats can't win, so its either Brown or Cameron.

Social Liberals and Economic Liberals

The Liberal Democrats describe their ideology as giving "power to the people". The Liberal Democrats are the party most in favour of devolution of political power away Westminster. The Liberal

Democrats were the most consistent supporters of the creation of a Scottish Parliament. The Liberal Democrats believe the answer to the famous "West Lothian Question" is the creating a federal United Kingdom, much like the federal system in the USA.

The Liberal Democrats are strong supporters of civil liberties. The party opposes the intervention of the state in individuals' private lives and has, for example, been a strong critic of some government anti-terrorist legislation and the proposals to introduce identity cards. Former Liberal leader, David Steel, became famous for his 1967 Private Members Bill which legalised abortion.

Simon Hughes MP is on the "social liberal" wing of the party.

The Liberal Democrats have some policies which would place the party to the left of Labour. The Liberal Democrats, unlike the Conservatives, opposed the war in Iraq. The Liberal Democrats are also in favour of raising taxes on the rich. The party's core vote lies with the educated middle classes. Famously derided as "Guardian readers", voters who care about "intellectual" issues such as the environment, proportional representation and equal opportunities are attracted to the Liberal Democrats.

One of the main problems for the Liberal Democrats in making a decisive political breakthrough is the First Past the Post electoral system. The party's voters are more dispersed around the country, rather than concentrated in specific areas. The party therefore finds it hard to translate its share of the vote into parliamentary seats. This then creates the problem of voters believing that a Liberal Democrat vote is a "wasted" vote. In recent years, the Liberal Democrats have tackled this problem by skillfully targeting seats and pursuing campaigns of "tactical voting". The Conservatives are vulnerable to many Liberal Democrat tactical campaigns, as the Liberal Democrats lie second in many Conservative held seats.

All parties have their internal divisions and the Liberal Democrats are no different. Given the party's famed openness and its opposition to "managerial" leadership, the Liberal Democrats have often been seen as a party which is impossible to lead. There are two identifiable "wings" of the Liberal Democrats; economic liberals and social liberals. Simon Hughes is a self proclaimed "social liberal". He could be placed on the party's left. Social Liberals are more likely to believe in state ownership of public services, increases in income tax for the rich and support for civil liberty issues.

On the "Right" are the so-called "Orange Book" economic liberals. Represented by Liberal Democrats such as Chris Huhne, the economic liberals believe in a more free market approach, with low taxes and private sector solutions.

Activities

- Why does the First Past the Post voting system make it difficult for the Liberal Democrats to win power?
- What is the Liberal Democrats dilemma as a centre party?
- What are the differences between social liberals and economic liberals?

The Rise of Scottish Nationalism

The SNP was formed in 1934 from the merger of the National Party of Scotland and the Scottish Party. The party largely avoided traditional Left/Right splits until the late 1970s. Then a party faction, the '79 group, which included in its ranks a young Alex Salmond, sought to give the party a more socialist identity. The '79 group was expelled, although most of its members later returned to the party as individuals.

As the Conservative Party lost its support in Scotland during the 1980s, the SNP emerged as the main challenger in Scotland to Labour. During this period, the party established its social democratic identity. The party's web site defines the SNP as "a democratic left-of-centre political party committed

to Scottish independence. It aims to create a just, caring and enterprising society by releasing Scotland's full potential as an independent nation in the mainstream of modern Europe".

The SNP's role models are the small nations of Northern Europe who have political independence and high standards of living. Finland and Sweden are often cited by the SNP as nations Scotland should aspire to. The recent success of the "Celtic Tiger" economy of the Republic of Ireland is used by Alex Salmond as evidence that an independent Scotland, within the European Union, can be successful. However, some left wing critics within the party have spoken of the low wages and wealth inequalities which also exist in the Republic of Ireland.

The SNP is enjoying its greatest political success since it won 11 MPs at the peak of the "It's Scotland's Oil" parliamentary campaign of 1974. The SNP forms a minority Scottish Government in the Scottish Parliament. It is also the largest party in Scottish local government. Electoral success brings party harmony. The SNP has had fractious inner-party relations in the past.

> The party's web site defines the SNP as "a democratic left-of-centre political party committed to Scottish independence. It aims to create a just, caring and enterprising society by releasing Scotland's full potential as an independent nation in the mainstream of modern Europe.

But, party unity is at an all-time high as the SNP basks in its historic defeat of Scottish Labour. There are, however, tensions imposed by the devolution settlement, and further tensions imposed by minority government within the settlement. In the recent past, there have been divisions within the SNP, between the so-called "fundamentalists" and the "gradualists". Fundamentalists" believe the devolution settlement

Scottish Cabinet meeting, May 2007. The SNP made a historic breakthrough in the 2007 Scottish Parliament elections.

to be a trap set by Unionist parties. They also feel the SNP leadership are prepared to downgrade the cause of Independence for more gradual "pro-Scottish" changes within the devolved settlement.

Former SNP MSP Campbell Martin is one such fundamentalist. He was expelled from the SNP for his outspoken criticism of then leader John Swinney. Jim Sillars, hero of the SNP's famous Govan by election win in 1988, could be categorised as a Fundamentalist too, as to a lesser extent could Alex Neil MSP, although he appears to have made his peace with the Salmond/Sturgeon leadership. N.B. So-called "fundamentalists" do not like this label, believing it to be a construct of the "pro-Unionist media".

The current leadership, who are very much on the gradualist wing of the party, see a minority SNP Scottish Government as a platform for independence. Alex Salmond's "long game" is to establish the SNP as a credible party of government. He believes this "try before you buy" approach will neuter the Unionist parties' attacks on the SNP as "wreckers". Salmond's aim for the 2007-2011 Scottish Parliament will be to have a successful SNP Government, within the limited powers the Scottish Parliament has under the Scotland Act.

This is not to say that independence as an aspiration has been "parked". First Minister Alex Salmond launched a "national conversation" on Scotland's constitutional status.

A white paper proposing a referendum on Scottish Independence has been presented in the Scottish Parliament. The name of the Scottish Executive has been changed to "The Scottish Government", as part of a psychological campaign to soften the Scottish public's opposition to full Scottish self-governance. Alex Salmond will try to win new powers for the Scottish Parliament, broadcasting being a prize goal, as part of a gradualist move towards full independence.

One of the problems facing the SNP's opponents' is the reasonableness of the SNP's demands! Alex Salmond has stated that a completely independent Scotland, led by the SNP, would keep the Queen as monarch. An SNP-led independent Scotland would also stick to interest rates set by the Bank of England.

Activities

- What is meant by the SNP's "try before you buy" approach to independence?
- In what ways is the SNP different from Scottish Labour?
- What political differences are there within the SNP?

Interview with Roseanna Cunningham MSP, Perth.

Modernity: Do you think there are any real ideological differences between the SNP and Scottish Labour?

Roseanna Cunningham: I think both parties are on the centre left of the political spectrum. The SNP, I would say is to the left of Labour as Labour in recent years have really moved into the centre. The SNP is a moderate, left of centre party.

We are more committed to doing things collectively. For example, we are opposed to Labour's use of Public Private Partnerships (PPPs) for public services. But, even this is more practical than ideological. We do not think they are good value for money. At the end of the PPP contract the public do not own the school or the hospital. But, now that these projects are up and running, local authorities which are SNP run will continue to work with the PPP. But, where it is not too late to stop a PPP we will. For example, the Cabinet Secretary for Justice (Kenny McAskill) recently stopped the building of a private jail.

Modernity: Other than Scottish independence, what is unique about SNP policies?

Roseanna Cunningham: We are very opposed to nuclear weapons, and Trident in particular due to its location in Scotland. The new Scottish Government hosted a Trident Summit in October 2007 to debate the issue. Traditionally, the SNP is also very much in favour of renewable energy and opposed to nuclear energy. In terms of foreign policy, the SNP has been against the war in Iraq.

Modernity: Can the SNP remain in government if independence is not a possibility?

Roseanna Cunningham: Let's watch this space! We now have a situation where the three main opposition parties are now congregating around a policy of increased powers for the Scottish Parliament. This is not what Scottish Labour was saying before the 2007 Scottish elections. Historically, the Conservatives had always been opposed to more powers. The Scottish Liberal Democrats may have been in favour, but because of the Partnership Agreement they couldn't discuss it.

So, the debate is now about more powers. Once

you start to address that logic, to me, the logic is inescapable. Independence may not happen tomorrow but the momentum is heading that way. We're prepared to put our arguments on independence to the people in a referendum. If the opposition parties are so confident of their arguments, why will they not agree to a referendum?

Modernity: Are there internal differences within the SNP?

Roseanna Cunningham: The SNP is a democratic political party so there are differences of opinion. There haven't been any formal factions within the SNP since the '79 group, which I was a part of some time ago. All in the SNP want independence but they are not all in the same place. Some people want to be more gradual in their approach than others. But, this debate has largely been overtaken by events, now that the Scottish Parliament is here.

The SNP, traditionally, has attracted members from across the political spectrum because they believe in independence. There is debate, which is healthy, but members accept the democratically agreed policies of the party.

Modernity: What is the policy making process within the SNP?

Roseanna Cunningham: Policy is made at the annual autumn party conference. SNP branches can send resolutions to conference and if there is support it can become party policy. In addition to conference, we have three national Councils during the year, which have much less media attention, but also decide party policy.

Ministers and spokespersons also deal with issues as they arise. This is the same in all political parties. But, these issues can be brought up again, either at National Council or party conference. There is healthy debate in the SNP. The SNP doesn't do deference!

Modernity: To what extent does the party leadership dominate policy making?

Roseanna Cunningham: The party leadership has more resources to draw on than party members. But, policy still has to be voted on. Local branches have talented and experienced members who can bring ideas to the table the leadership may not. For example, Professor Neil McCormick is a party member, but he is also a much respected professor in public law at Edinburgh University. If he has a policy idea, it is not just the SNP leadership who will listen, but leaders of other political parties too.

"Independence may not happen tomorrow but the momentum is heading that way. We're prepared to put our arguments on independence to the people in a referendum. If the opposition parties are so confident of their arguments, why will they not agree to a referendum?"

Chapter 7 Internal Affairs

Party Structures: Conservative Party

The leader of the Conservative Party has a very prominent role in decision making within the party. The leader is expected to take into account the views of party members, his front bench spokespersons and the parliamentary back benchers, who are represented by the 1922 Committee (the famous men in grey suits). The Conservatives are much more of a "top down" organisation than the other political parties.

While famously ruthless at removing unsuccessful leaders, the Conservatives place great trust and power in a leader they like to feel is in control.
The leader alone decides on the make up of the Cabinet or Shadow Cabinet. The Conservative leader has responsibility for writing the party's election manifestos. The leader appoints the party Chairman, who is in charge of Conservative Central Office in London. Unlike the Labour Party, the Conservative Party conference has absolutely no formal powers to make party policy. The Conservative Party conference is more of a networking opportunity than a decision making body. Delegates attend to "press flesh" with key party people and to show support for the party leadership.

This is not to say that the Conservative party conference does not have any significance. Party leaders often use the conference as an opportunity to launch new policy ideas. A bad, or good, conference speech can have enormous implications for a Conservative politician's political future. David Cameron made his pitch for the party leadership at the 2005 party conference. He almost certainly saved his leadership by his speech at the 2007 party conference.

The A-list

Until William Hague's reforms of 1998, Conservative constituency associations had complete freedom in the selection of party candidates. This was good for the morale of activists as they felt involved in decision making. However, a disadvantage was that Conservative party parliamentary candidates tended to come from similar backgrounds. Overwhelmingly male, affluent, middle aged and white, Conservative MPs did not reflect the country they sought to govern. 91% of Conservative MPs are men. At the 2005 General Election, women were selected in only six of the party's top 50 winnable seats and only 17 Tory women were elected overall - 8.6% of the parliamentary party.

David Cameron is trying to make the Conservative Party more attractive to a diverse range of voters. Photo opportunities with Nelson Mandela can't do the Conservatives any harm.

This compares with Labour's 98 female MPs (27.5%). Two ethnic minority Conservative candidates were elected, both men.
In an attempt to broaden the party's appeal, David Cameron has attempted to create a more diverse pool of talent for local parties to choose their parliamentary candidates from.

In 2006, Cameron created the "A-list". Constituency Conservative associations in the party's 200 most winnable seats can only select candidates who have been included on the A-List, compiled by Conservative Central Office. Only in "exceptional circumstances" can constituency associations consider

other outstanding local candidates. Younger, female, candidates were encouraged to apply for membership of the A-List, as were ethnic minorities.

The A-list has sparked both public and private protests. Adam Rickitt, a former Coronation Street actor, was favoured over more experienced candidates. Male candidates, especially, have felt discriminated against.
Cameron's A-List is reminiscent of Labour's positive discrimination campaign in the early 1990s. In order to increase the number of female Labour representatives, constituency Labour parties could only choose candidates from female only shortlists.

This policy was abandoned following a legal challenge on the grounds of sex discrimination. By the time the issue was resolved many more women had been selected as parliamentary candidates. After Labour's landslide election victory in 1997, 101 female Labour MPs were elected. The Representation of the Peoples Act (Election Candidates) Act 2002 enabled Labour to allow all women shortlists again. Twenty two of the new Labour MPs elected in 2005 were women. David Cameron has vowed to introduce all women shortlists if the Conservative Party resists the A-List.

In 2006, BBC's Newsnight programme compiled background information on 100 of David Cameron's A-list. 46% of the Newsnight 100 were women. The Newsnight 100 also revealed an increase in the number of candidates from ethnic minorities. However, in terms of their social class background, 52% of the Newsnight 100 were privately educated.

This compares with 59% of the Conservative MPs elected in 2005 who were privately educated. 28% of the Newsnight 100 went to Oxford or Cambridge. Two-thirds of the Newsnight 100 worked in the world of business, media and politics. 18% came from a financial background; 17% politics; 17% media, PR and campaigning and 14% from private business. Nine were lawyers, six per cent were medics and three worked in education. The rest came from a mixed bag, ranging from the Metropolitan Police and the Ministry of Sound to farming and the stage.

> **Activities**
>
> • What is the role of the Conservative party leader?
> • What is the role of the Conservative Party conference?
> • What was David Cameron's A List designed to achieve?
> • To what extent has the A-list been successful?

Party Structures: Liberal Democrats

Nicol Stephen MSP, Aberdeen South. Leader of the Scottish Liberal Democrats

The Liberal Democrats have a federal structure, with each of the party's national organisations given considerable freedoms to decide policy in their respective areas. The Scottish Liberal Democrats are one of the 3 state parties within the federal structure of the British Liberal Democrats; the others being the English and the Welsh parties. The federal structure can result in the Scottish and Welsh Liberal Democrats having different policies in their areas of responsibility.

In keeping with its basis as a federation of organisations, the Scottish party is composed of 8 regional parties. These regions are based on the boundaries of the 8 Scottish Parliament electoral regions which are broken down into local party organisations following the boundaries of the 73 Scottish Parliament constituencies.

Unlike the other major parties, the Liberal Democrats have two national conferences. In spring and autumn, elected representatives from Liberal Democrat constituency parties assemble at the party conference to establish federal party policy. Federal policy covers those areas that would fall within the remit of the federal institutions of a federal United Kingdom. England, Scotland and Wales set their own policies for their own areas.

Party Structures: Labour

Policy making in the Labour Party, like much else in the party, has been "modernised" in recent years. Labour Party conferences used to be fiery affairs. The Labour leadership would be accused of betrayal to the socialist cause by ideologically motivated conference delegates and trade union leaders. Policy would be debated in an often confrontational manner and the wider world watching on television would wonder why the protagonists were members of the same political party.

Those days are gone. Today's Labour Party conference is highly professional and very stage managed. Conference is no longer about making policy, but is instead about celebrating the party leadership. Labour paid a high price for its disunity in the 1980s and it has no wish to, as former leader Neil Kinnock put it, "wash its dirty laundry in public".

> "Conference has long ceased to be the driver of debate within the Labour Party." Martin Bright, Political Editor, New Statesman

Prior to 1997, delegates to conference would submit motions to discuss. A party management group would select motions which would be put before conference. Policy in the Labour Party is now made through a process called Partnership in Power (PiP). PiP is based around a rolling series of consultations involving Policy Forums made up of individual party members, trade unionists and other affiliated organisations. The Policy Forums report to the National Policy Forum (NPF) which publishes its Annual report. This is delivered to the annual conference and the party leadership has responsibility to act on its advice.

The new system certainly takes the heat out of debates. Policy is now debated more fully and over a longer period of time. The hand of the party leadership is also strengthened. The opportunity for individuals or small groups of unrepresentative members to win a one off conference vote has been taken away. If there are policies in the NPF which the leadership does not care for, these can be discarded.

This however has de-motivated some Labour Party activists. They feel that the NPF can simply cherry pick the ideas it likes and ignore the ones it doesn't. It takes a lot of time and effort to attend Policy Forum meetings and if these do not result in a change of policy, activists can lose interest.

Activities

- What is meant by the Liberal Democrat's federal party structure?
- Why did Labour move away from delegates being able to make policy directly at the party conference?
- Why have some party members been critical of Partnership in Power?

Leadership Elections: Conservative

In the past, Conservative leaders were not elected. They "emerged" from within a small group of usually male and usually aristocratic MPs. By contrast, recent years have seen several elections for the party leadership, each of them having complex rules over voting procedures.

The Conservatives, in their quest to defeat New Labour, have had five leaders in the past ten years: John Major, William Hague, Iain Duncan Smith, Michael Howard and now David Cameron, as many as the party had had in the previous forty years.

David Cameron won the 2005 leadership election against his rivals Kenneth Clark, David Davis and Liam Fox. The election was fought under the rules introduced by previous leader, William Hague.

Lord Tebbit, above, is concerned that the Cameron leadership has lost sight of "traditional" Conservative values.

The rules for election of the Conservative leader are as follows:

Candidates present themselves to the backbench 1922 Committee. If there are more than two candidates, which there were in 2005, Conservative MPs vote in order to eliminate the lowest placed candidates. Kenneth Clarke gained fewest votes, he was eliminated. There remained three candidates, so a second ballot among MPs took place to narrow the field down to two. Liam Fox this time finished bottom and he was eliminated. A ballot among party members therefore took place to decide who the leader of the Conservatives should be. David Cameron won 134,446 votes on a 78% turnout, beating David Davis's 64,398 votes.

Cameron won the leadership of his party because he offered something different. He promised to make the Conservatives part of mainstream British society. In many ways his pitch was similar to that of Tony Blair's. He promised to modernise party organisation and campaigning and bring policies back into the centre ground. His critics on the more traditionalist wing of the party believe that he is abandoning "core" Conservative values.

Cameron, however, is pursuing the tried and tested politics of "narrow casting" his political message. Narrow casting is similar to the big tent approach. He is sending out a signal to the country at large that his party has a new agenda.

He is doing this by way of his language, his symbolism (for example, the new green and blue party logo) and carefully managed media events (his trip to Norway's glaciers). The Cameron-led Conservatives now care about "social breakdown". They care about the environment. At the same time, to reassure Conservative grassroots, the party continues to talk tough about Britain's role in Europe. Despite the talk of "hugging a hoody", tough sentences are promised for offenders.

Activities

- Describe the process of electing a leader in the Conservative Party.
- Why did the Conservative Party choose David Cameron as party leader?
- What is meant by "narrow casting"?

Leadership Elections: Labour

Labour has not had a leadership election since 1994. Gordon Brown was elected unopposed as Labour leader after left wing candidate, John McDonnell failed to win the support of 20% of Labour MPs which is required under the party's rules to contest a leadership election.

Gordon Brown was elected Labour leader unopposed in June 2007.

In 1994 Gordon Brown famously chose not to run for leadership of the Labour Party, allowing his friend Tony Blair to run instead. Legend has it that in an Islington restaurant Blair promised Brown that if he was elected as Prime Minister, Brown would be his Chancellor, but for one term only. After that he would stand down and "allow" Brown to take over as leader. The deal, if there was one, never materialised. Gordon Brown was the longest-serving Chancellor in living memory. He has waited a long time to be Labour leader and Prime Minister.

Labour has quite a different process from the Conservatives for electing its leader. The decision lies with an electoral college, split equally three ways between the 354 Labour MPs and the Labour MEPs, all party members and members of affiliated trade unions who continue to pay a political levy. If any candidate receives a majority of votes, they are declared the leader. If not, the last placed contender drops out and their second preferences arereallocated

- and so on until someone passes the 50% figure.

Gordon Brown's leadership brought a rush of funds into the party. Almost £500,000 was donated in the first three days of Gordon Brown taking over as Prime Minister. Labour traditionally receives the bulk of its funding from trade unions. However, as the party has become increasingly business friendly, donations from private individuals and firms have been well received. Among the new donors to Labour are the online betting company, Bet 365, and Sir Ronald Cohen, a leading private equity businessman.

Labour needs the funds. The party is estimated to be £16 million in debt, while the Conservatives are around £9 million in debt. Labour has been wounded by the Metropolitan Police's "Cash for Honours" enquiry.

Allegations had been made that Labour's chief fundraiser, Lord Levy, had, in dalliance with Prime Minister Tony Blair, offered seats in the House of Lords to those who gave donations or loans to the Labour Party. Lord Levy was arrested, re-arrested, bailed and re-bailed, on charges of breaking the 1925 Honours (Prevention of Abuses) Act and on suspicion of perverting the course of justice.

The Crown's case collapsed due to an inability to prove that "commercial deals" had been struck. Yet, Cash for Honours remains a problem for Gordon Brown. Labour Party membership is at its lowest point in history. Labour is in more debt now than it was before the 2005 General Election. Gordon Brown will not be able to call upon "Lord Cashpoint", as Lord Levy became known, to raise the millions needed for future election campaigns.

Activities

- What was the deal Tony Blair allegedly made with Gordon Brown in 1994?
- In what ways are Labour Party leadership elections different from Conservative leadership elections?
- In what ways has the Cash for Honours scandal affected the Labour Party?

Leadership Elections: Liberal Democrats

Menzies Campbell was elected leader of the Liberal Democrats on 3 March 2006. He resigned less than a year and a half later, without fighting a General Election as leader. Previous leader Charles Kennedy stood down after allegations about his personal life. Campbell successfully saw off competition for the post from Simon Hughes, a social liberal, and Chris Huhne, from the more pro business wing of the party.

Elections for the Liberal Democrat leader are, as one might expect, carried out by proportional representation. Election is by STV in a secret ballot. Candidates, who must be MPs, must be supported by 10% of the Parliamentary Party and by at least 200 members representing at least 20 local parties. After the first ballot in 2006, Simon Hughes was eliminated, leaving a straight contest between Menzies Campbell and Chris Huhne.

Menzies Campbell won, securing 57.86% of the vote. This was not an overwhelming mandate and Campbell never managed to win over all sections of the party. All Liberal Democrat party members are entitled to vote in a leadership election. Menzies Campbell did not have the easiest of times as leader. Elected leader because of his gravitas and respect amongst the public, there was the expectation that he would make the electoral breakthrough where Charles Kennedy had failed.

The Liberal Democrats felt that the party, with its popular anti Iraq war stance, could have done much better in the 2005 General Election. Kennedy was criticised for being lethargic and complacent in campaigning. Menzies Campbell was criticised for allowing Conservative leader, David Cameron, to seize the media agenda and centre ground votes away from the Liberal Democrats.

At the 2007 autumn party conference, Campbell responded to his critics' complaints about his age stating that, rather than not allowing age to be a factor, he would make age an issue. Unfortunately for Campbell, with Gordon Brown postponing a General Election until 2009 and the Liberal Democrats trailing badly in the opinion polls, party activists put sufficient pressure on Menzies Campbell to resign. Less than a month after receiving a standing ovation at the party conference, he was gone.

Activities

- Describe the process of electing a Liberal Democrat party leader.
- What criticisms have been made about recent Liberal Democrat leaders?

The Scottish Dimension

The Scottish Conservatives

In Scotland, the Scottish Conservatives elected Annabelle Goldie as Scottish leader in 2005. Previous Scottish leader, David McLetchie, was forced to resign after a scandal involving inappropriate claims of taxi expenses for Scottish parliamentary business. Journalists took an interest in McLetchie after he hounded Labour First Minister Henry McLeish into resigning in 2001. They used Freedom of Information laws to unearth details of his £11,500 taxi bill, the highest of any MSP for the first five years of the parliament. Annabel Goldie, a "safe pair of hands", was subsequently elected as leader, unopposed, on a joint platform with Murdo Fraser as her Deputy Leader.

The Scottish Conservatives faced serious ideological difficulties with the creation of the Scottish parliament. The most Unionist of all the UK parties, the Scottish Conservatives had opposed both the setting up of the parliament and its additional member voting system. Yet, it has been the additional member system that has, arguably, kept the Conservatives alive in Scottish politics. The

Conservative party nationally also made the decision to grant the Scottish party considerable freedom to set policies which may be different from the UK party to help it build a more "Scottish" identity. Part of the Conservatives' problem in Scotland was their identification with an "English" agenda and the perception thatthey were unsympathetic to the specific economic needs of Scotland.

David McLetchie MSP, Edinburgh Pentlands. Mr McLetchie had to resign as Scottish Conservative leader in 2005 following allegations over misuse of parliamentary expenses.

The party now has its own Scottish Conservative Central Office, under the leadership of David Mundell. The Scottish Conservatives hold their own annual party conference. The Scottish party writes its own manifesto for Scottish Parliament elections. In 2007, it advocated that the Scottish Parliament should cut income tax, whereas the UK-based party has not committed itself to tax cuts. Annabel Goldie attempted to make criminal justice a vote winner. She supported the abolition of Scotland's "double jeopardy" system to convict those who, in the light of new evidence, had escaped justice in their initial court trial.

Annabel Goldie commands respect across the political divide for her combative, yet personable, debating style. She will have been disappointed that the Scottish Conservatives were unable to rise above the 14% of the vote that the party appears to have bottomed out at. Realistically, the days of the Conservative Party running Scotland appear to be gone. But, given the Scottish Conservatives' remarkably good relations with the SNP, a future coalition may not be as impossible as seemed.

Scottish Liberal Democrats

Scottish Liberal Democrat policy is set at the party's two annual conferences, and Welsh policy is set through the Welsh Conferences. English policy, and policy with wider applicability across the UK, is debated at the federal party conferences. Every year, conference representatives elect a Federal Policy Committee (FPC) which is responsible for the production of the policy papers that are debated by Conference. The FPC is also responsible for election manifestos.

Party members discuss policy papers in local and regional meetings, and their representatives then debate and vote on policy motions and papers at Conference. Conference also debates motions submitted by local parties and conference representatives. The FPC is chaired by the party leader. The FPC decides the party's General Election manifesto, in consultation with the parliamentary Liberal Democrats.

Nicol Stephen replaced Jim Wallace as Scottish leader of the Liberal Democrats in May 2005. He defeated his rival, Mike Rumbles, who had advocated ending the Scottish Liberal Democrats coalition with Labour in the Scottish Executive. Nicol Stephen served as Deputy First Minister between 2005 and 2007. When Nicol Stephen took over as leader, he was a bit of an unknown quantity. He still is. In

Because of the Liberal Democrats' federal structure, the Scottish party has considerable scope to devise its own policy, which can be different from that of the other national Liberal Democrats. It was the Scottish Liberal Democrats who took the decision not to enter into coalition with the SNP after the 2007 Scottish elections.

a poll for the Times newspaper in April 2007, only 7% of Scottish voters said he would make the best First Minister.

Because of the Liberal Democrats' federal structure, the Scottish party has considerable scope to devise its own policy, which can be different from that of the other national Liberal Democrats. It was the Scottish Liberal Democrats who took the decision not to enter into coalition with the SNP after the 2007 Scottish elections. Nicol Stephen told the Liberal Democrat 2007 autumn conference that the Scottish Liberal Democrats are in favour of the Scottish Parliament ending its block grant from Westminster and assuming full tax raising powers.

Activities

- What is the role of the Liberal Democrat's Federal Policy Committee?
- What evidence is there of the Scottish Liberal Democrats pursuing a distinctively Scottish approach?

The Scottish Labour Party

Two key players in Scottish Labour: Jack McConnell and Andy Kerr. East Kilbride, 2006.

Conference decides in the second year which of the policy proposals to adopt as party policy.

Labour's "Scottishness" has been an issue for the party in a similar way to the Conservatives. Scottish Labour has sought to emphasise its "Scottishness", yet within a British context. Scottish Labour believes that the "partnership" between Scottish and UK organisations, in government as well as party politics, provides Scotland with the best of both worlds.

The downside for Scottish Labour is that, if the party is unpopular at a UK level, for example over the war in Iraq, or over "Cash for Honours", it is difficult for the Scottish organisation to disassociate itself. The advantage of the UK connection is partly financial, but should a Labour Prime Minister be popular, the Scottish party can use this association to promote the virtues of partnership, rather than "separation", with the UK.

Jack McConnell famously sought "Scottish solutions for Scottish problems". Wendy Alexander replaced Jack McConnell as Labour's leader in the Scottish Parliament after the party's defeat at the 2007 Scottish Parliament election. Like Jack McConnell, and his predecessor Henry McLeish, Wendy Alexander did not face competition for the leadership post. Scottish Labour is having to come to terms with opposition. Opposition does not come easily to a party accustomed to power. At the Labour Party's 2007 conference, Wendy Alexander took the unusual step of apologising to the party for Scottish Labour losing the elections. She has promised a "root and branch" review of the party's policies and pledged that Scottish Labour will "re-connect" with the voters.

In September 2007, she unveiled a new 'virtual' policy think tank to generate fresh thinking on Scottish Labour policy. 'Ideas Scotland' will be run by Oxford University academic Gregg McClymont

The Scottish Labour Party is the devolved party of the UK Labour Party. It holds a bi-annual party conference where policy is made which it believes will appeal to Scottish voters. Policy is made by Scottish Labour's Scottish Policy Forum (SPF). The Scottish Policy Forum operates on a two-year programme. At the end of the first year, consultation documents are presented to Scottish Conference. At the end of the second year, the SPF presents policy proposals to conference. These may include majority and minority reports with different policy positions.

and will not be dominated by the Scottish Labour leadership. It will seek to involve key experts, spokespersons from pressure groups and the wider public in its attempts to renew Labour thinking on devolved matters.

Activities

- In what ways has the Scottish Labour Party faced problems over its national identity?
- Why can Scottish Labour's partnership with the UK Labour Party be both an advantage and a disadvantage?
- What are Wendy Alexander's priorities as Labour's leader in the Scottish Parliament?

Scottish National Party

The SNP, like all political parties, is proud of the role played by local members in local party branches. SNP branches form an association in the parliamentary constituency they represent. There are also 8 regional associations, corresponding to the 8 Scottish Parliament regions to which the branches and constituency associations can send delegates. The SNP's policy structure is developed at its annual National Conference and its regular National Council meetings. Branches can submit resolutions to the National Conference, and if passed, these will become party policy.

The SNP has an active youth section as well as a student section. There is also, in an attempt to break into Labour's working class core vote, an SNP Trade Union Group. There is an independently-owned monthly newspaper, The Scots Independent, which is highly supportive of the party.

The SNP's leadership is its National Executive Committee (NEC), which is made up of the party's elected office bearers and 10 members who are elected at the party's national conference. The SNP's parliamentarians (Scottish, Westminster and European) and councillors have representation on the NEC, as do the Trade Union Group and the youth wing/student wing jointly.

SNP party membership has grown considerably in recent times, especially since the party has become one of government. Party managers claim SNP membership has grown by 8 per cent since the end of 2006. In June 2007, the SNP had 13,585 members, compared to a total of 12,571 at the end of December. For a long time, the SNP was a poor relation in Scottish politics. The unionist parties such as Labour and Conservative could rely on UK-wide funds from their trade union and business backers. While the SNP continues to find difficulty in campaigning for local, Scottish, UK and European elections, party finances have been helped by donations from high profile Scots such as Brian Souter (head of Stagecoach buses) and Sir Sean Connery.

Alex Salmond was elected leader of the SNP, for the second time, in 2004. Salmond resigned as leader in 2000 to be replaced by John Swinney. At the time, Salmond stated that ten years was "long enough" to be party leader, and it was time for someone else to do the job. As an MP, he remained leader of the SNP at Westminster. When John Swinney resigned as party leader it was a surprise to many that Alex Salmond stood again for the post. He had been asked on several occasions whether he would stand again for the party's leadership. He famously replied; "If nominated I'll decline. If drafted I'll defer. And if elected I'll resign."

Yet, in 2004 he stood again, despite not being a member of the Scottish Parliament. His election campaign promised that, if elected, his close ally Nicola Sturgeon would act as a temporary leader in the Scottish Parliament (giving her valuable experience as a potential future SNP leader), while he would be leader in the country at large. He would aim to win a seat in the Scottish Parliament at the 2007 Scottish elections. The leadership contest took place in September 2004. Alex Salmond won by an overwhelming majority (75% of the vote) against his two challengers; Roseanna Cunningham, who came

When asked if he would stand again to be SNP leader, Alex Salmond famously replied "If nominated I'll decline. If drafted I'll defer. And if elected I'll resign.

Alex Salmond completed an amazing political comeback by winning the Scottish Parliamentary seat of Gordon.

second, and Mike Russell. All SNP members were entitled to vote in a postal ballot.

Alex Salmond at the time claimed that he was not just standing to be SNP leader but to become Scotland's First Minister as well. In order to do so, he first had to find a Scottish Parliamentary constituency to stand in, then win the election.

The party also had to beat Scottish Labour in a country-wide election, something the SNP had never achieved in its 73-year history. Salmond stood in the Gordon constituency where he achieved an almost 19% swing, beating the Scottish Liberal Democrat MSP Nora Radcliffe. The SNP also famously won the 2007 Scottish Parliament elections.

Due to Salmond's political skills and his command of the party, the SNP has been criticised as being a "one man band". While Salmond is in some respects one of the few "big hitters" in the Scottish Parliament, it is evident that his capable Deputy Leader, Nicola Sturgeon, has been groomed for future leadership of the party.

The phenomenal rise in support in SNP membership would indicate that, if the party can continue its success, there will be a new generation of career-oriented party activists ready for leadership in future years.

Activities

- Describe the policy making process within the SNP.
- Why is the SNP no longer the poor relation of Scottish politics?
- Why is the SNP sometimes criticised as a being a "one man band"?

Chapter 8
Policies and Electoral Success

Conservative Party Policies

In December 2005, David Cameron set up a wide-ranging policy review. He created six different groups, each being given the scope to "think the unthinkable". David Cameron has stated that the recommendations of the groups would not necessarily be adopted as Tory policy. But the findings will feed into the party's decision making process ahead of a General Election.

Many of these policies became a little more "fleshed out" at the 2007 party conference as the party believed a General Election was imminent.

The main recommendations of each group are as follows:

Social Justice
· Increase taxes on beer and wine to battle binge drinking
· Increase working tax credits for married couples
· Reclassify cannabis back upwards as a dangerous drug

National and International Security
· A dedicated UK border force
· Push Muslim community organisations to allow women into their leadership structures

Globalisation and Global Poverty
· Remove trade barriers to the developing world
· Increase the proportion of aid spent on economic development
· Only offer training (as opposed to work) to medical staff from developing countries to avoid brain drain

Economic Competitiveness
· Scrap inheritance tax (which brings in £4bn a year

for the Treasury)
· Cut corporation tax to 25p
· Abolish capital gains tax on assets held for more than 10 years
· Repeal working time regulations

Public Service Improvement
· State aid worth 10% of the value of their home to help council tenants buy a property
· A national fund for affordable housing in areas where it is needed

Quality of Life
· Increase taxes on short-haul domestic flights including the introduction of VAT
· Introduce a high registration tax for gas-guzzling cars and give VAT relief to smaller, cleaner cars
· Ban environmentally unfriendly electrical goods and those that remain on standby when switched off.

Shadow Chancellor George Osborne put Labour on the defensive with his inheritance tax plans. Conservative Party conference, October 2007.

The headline policy of the Conservatives at the party's 2007 conference was the unveiling of a new tax plan. Over the past few years, as house prices have soared, many "middle England" voters are now paying so called stealth taxes, such as Inheritance Tax which used to be reserved only for the very rich. Inheritance Tax is paid by those with assets worth more than £250,000. Many homes are now worth considerably more than £250,000.

Shadow Chancellor George Osborne outlined his plans to raise the Inheritance Tax threshold to £1 million. It would be funded by a new tax on non domiciles, those who work in the UK but pay little tax because they do not live here. Chelsea Football Club chairman Ramon Abramovich is probably the most famous "non dom", although there are thousands more. The Conservatives plan to tax non-

doms £25,000 per year.

In education, the Conservatives have five headline policies: restore classroom discipline, cut teachers' paperwork, give parents greater choice, fund new school places and scrap university tuition fees. Shadow Children's Minister, the self-declared One Nation Conservative, Michael Gove, introduced the party's new campaign *Comprehensively Excellent*, "in which we identify some of the very best state schools in the country and identify the qualities which help make them a success." The Conservatives were seeking to explain why they support the state sector yet support parental choice, high standards and good discipline within it.

On Europe, traditionally a deal breaker for party unity, the Conservatives appeared to agree not to disagree with one another for once. David Cameron said Britain would "get out of the European Social Chapter", so that employment rules and worker rights can be made in Britain, not the European Union (EU).

This is a reassertion of a previous Conservative policy that was actually dropped in 2004, on the grounds it was no longer practical. Labour signed up to the European Social Chapter in 1997. Ministers say that for a future UK government to opt out again, it would require the agreement of the rest of the EU, which is unlikely to be forthcoming. Party activists were more excited by Shadow Foreign Secretary William Hague's promise of a referendum, not just on the proposed EU reform treaty, but on any future accord that transfers power to the EU.

On law and order, Shadow Home Secretary David Davis pledged to end an early release scheme for prisoners and cut immigration. This was classic, traditional Conservatism and the type of policy commitment activists, suspicious of David Cameron's "hug a hoody" reputation, wanted to hear. David Davis said he would use savings, from ditching the identity card programme, to pay for the expansion of prisons. He said that under a Conservative government police would "reclaim the streets" and "break up the gangs". "They will enforce zero-tolerance of all crime." David Davis would not commit himself on any numbers in relation to cuts in immigration.

Labour

Tony Blair promised that, as the party was elected as New Labour, it would govern as New Labour. Tony Blair had won a power struggle against Gordon Brown to become Prime Minister. He quickly made Brown his Chancellor of the Exchequer, a post he was to keep for much longer than he expected. It was important for New Labour to establish a reputation for financial "prudence". Up until "black Wednesday" in September 1992, the Conservatives had been the party with the reputation for economic competence. The Conservatives lost it, and Gordon Brown doesn't want to give them it back.

Gordon Brown has been responsible for New Labour economic policy. His first policy decision was to hand over operational decisions to the Bank of England. Decisions over interest rates would no longer be a political tool which could be used by a Chancellor, but "apolitical" decisions taken by an "independent" authority. With growing numbers of people borrowing money and owning their homes, decisions over interest rates are now highly important.

Gordon Brown also committed Labour to low direct taxation. The basic rate of Income Tax, which most workers pay, has been reduced by Gordon Brown to 20%. This is the headline figure and what most voters recognise. However, with growing prosperity, many middle income voters now pay a section of their earnings at the higher rate of tax, which has remained at 40%. These decisions pleased New Labour supporters. But record spending on health and education (these powers were devolved to the Scottish Parliament) pleased traditional Labour supporters.

As part of its plans to "modernise" the fabric of schools and hospitals, New Labour supported "public private partnerships" (PPPs). PPPs mean that new schools can be built, or renovated, without the Government having to pay upfront. Instead, a private company, or consortium of companies, pays for the construction and the maintenance. The

The new Williamwood High School, East Renfrewshire, a Public Private Partnership.

In his leader's speech to the 2007 Labour Party conference, Gordon Brown used the word "Britain" 52 times, "British" 28 times and "children" 27 times. "Blair" was mentioned three times and "Iraq" once.

Government rents the school for a period of, usually, thirty years. During this time, the private company owns the building and pays for any maintenance. At the end of the period, the Government can choose to either buy the school at an agreed fee or continue to rent.

PPPs have enabled New Labour to build many schools which may have been impossible under more traditional ways of spending. Critics however claim that PPPs represent a "buy now, pay later" approach which is more expensive in the long term than "old fashioned" government borrowing.

At the 2007 Labour Party conference, a crime and disorder policy based on the principle of "punish and prevent" was unveiled. The Prime Minister outlined a series of measures including increased powers to the police to stop and search. There will be a minimum five year sentence for carrying a gun. Home Secretary Jacqui Smith and Jack Straw the Justice Minister were determined to outflank the Conservatives on their traditional territory of "law and order". Smith and Straw's zero tolerance agenda includes issuing the police with mobile weapon detectors and mobile finger print machines in order to target low level crime in the community.

The focal point of Labour's conference these days however is the leader's speech. Gordon Brown planned his speech as a starting gun in an election campaign. Speaking to Conservative voters watching on television news bulletins rather than to Labour activists in the hall (the conference stage backdrop changed to blue when he got up to speak), Brown committed Labour to "aspiration and meritocracy". In his speech he used the word "Britain" 52 times, "British" 28 times and "children" 27 times. "Blair" was mentioned three times and "Iraq" once.

Activities

- To what extent has Gordon Brown governed as New Labour?
- What are the key New Labour economic policies?
- Why has Gordon Brown emphasised his British identity?

Scottish National Party

The nationalist historian Tom Nairn jokingly stated that Scotland would only be reborn when the last Church of Scotland Minister was strangled with the last copy of the Sunday Post. Nairn was referring to Scotland's then conservative political culture and the influence of the highly conservative Sunday Post newspaper.

Times have changed. The Church of Scotland was to the fore of the campaign for a Scottish Parliament. Indeed, while the Holyrood Scottish Parliament building was being constructed, the parliament met at the Church of Scotland's General Assembly. The Conservatives now battle with the Scottish Liberal Democrats for third place in Scottish politics. And Oor Wullie and Daphne Broon are hardly role models for today's teenagers.

The SNP has changed too. For a long time, the SNP was a marginal force in Scottish politics. The party achieved rare General Election success, the February 1974 election being the exception. There were occasional by-election breakthroughs, two in Glasgow Govan in 1973 and 1988, both of which amounted to false dawns.

During these years, the SNP was attempting to find an identity for itself. It was for Scottish independence, but what else? Short of full Scottish independence, what did the SNP stand for? It was unlikely that voters would vote for independence without sampling what SNP government, either at local or national level, would mean. The SNP therefore gradually fashioned policies which would, on the one hand, be deliverable without Scottish independence, yet at the same time it would also campaign for full independence.

The SNP refused to participate in the Scottish Constitutional Convention (SCC) which set up the Scottish Parliament. The SNP was very wary of the SCC, which it saw as being dominated by the Scottish Labour Party and other pro Unionist organisations. The SCC was never going to put independence as an option to the voters, so the SNP decided to boycott the discussions. While the SNP had been making gains at a local government level, the elections to the Scottish Parliament, with the more proportional Additional Member System, gave the party its big breakthrough. Between 1999 and 2003, the SNP became the official opposition and in May 2007, the party took office as the Scottish Government for the first time.

The SNP remains committed to its long term goal of Scottish independence within the European Union.

Scottish independence remains the party's goal. It believes that Scotland cannot fulfil its potential unless the Scottish Parliament has full powers over taxation, defence and all the other powers of sovereign nations. To this end, First Minister Alex Salmond has embarked on a "National Conversation" about the country's constitutional future.

Alex Salmond is also keen to have broadcasting devolved to Scotland. He has set up a Broadcasting Commission, composed of eminent Scottish broadcasting experts and personalities. Alex Salmond is also keen to neuter Labour charges that an SNP Government would be irresponsible with the country's finances. The First Minister has set up a "National Economic Council", with respected economists and businessmen, to advise on how to boost Scotland's economic growth and performance. The SNP is committed to an independent Scotland being a full member state of the European Union, as well as supporting Scottish entry to the single European currency at the appropriate exchange rate.

It is important to distinguish between the SNP's

long-term and short-term goals. Independence is the long-term goal. The 2007 SNP manifesto promised a referendum on independence by 2011. However, the party's tiny parliamentary majority means such a referendum is highly unlikely. Alex Salmond therefore has to be patient and play a "long game". He will first of all seek to build on the SNP's first ever Scottish election win by establishing the party's reputation for sound economic management and good government. At the same time, he will both push for more powers of the Scottish Government and try to create a political mood in which the values of Scottish independence can flourish. This explains why Alex Salmond changed the name of the Scottish Executive to the Scottish Government.

Short term party policies include the party's plans to abolish the Council Tax and replace it with a Local Income Tax. This Local Income Tax differs from the Scottish Liberal Democrats' Local Income Tax in the sense that the SNP's tax would be the same for all living in Scotland. The Scottish Liberal Democrats Local Income Tax would instead be set by each of Scotland's 32 local authorities, as Council Tax is at present. The SNP Local Income Tax has been estimated at an additional 3p on income tax for all tax payers.

Activities

- What changes took place in Scottish society and politics to enable the SNP to become a serious political force?
- How has the SNP been able to persuade voters that it is a credible party of government without Scottish independence?
- In what ways has First Minister Alex Salmond tried to create the conditions for full Scottish independence?

Liberal Democrats

The Liberal Democrats are mature enough to appreciate that it is unlikely they will be able to form a government, due to the nature of the UK's First Past the Post electoral system. The best the party can hope for is to be "kingmaker" in a hung parliament, and make the introduction of Proportional Representation (PR) the price of any coalition partnership.

Vincent Cable MP, branded Gordon Brown, the "patron saint of the super rich".

The Scottish Liberal Democrats made the introduction of the Single Transferable Vote (STV) to Scottish local elections a non-negotiable part of its coalition with Scottish Labour in the Scottish Parliament. However, the Liberal Democrats appear to have now dropped a demand for the introduction of PR as a pre-condition of any coalition agreement. At the Liberal Democrats' 2007 spring party conference, former leader Menzies Campbell set out his "five tests" to Prime Minister Gordon Brown, which amounted to the five priorities for any Labour/ Liberal Democrat coalition. These are

- More civil liberties
- More policies to tackle global warming
- More power to local authorities and communities
- More efforts to tackle poverty
- More independence from the USA in British foreign policy

At the party's 2007 autumn conference the Liberal Democrats, perhaps expecting a snap General Election, spelled out in more detail what some of their policies were. Vincent Cable branded Gordon Brown "the patron saint of the super rich". The party unveiled a new tax policy which would cut the

basic rate of income tax by 4p in the pound. This would be funded by an increase in income tax for the rich, green taxes on aircraft and the most polluting vehicles. Cable argued that 90% of households would be better off, but that households earning more than £68,000 per year could be worse off.

Activities

- What is the Liberal Democrats' main hope for a political breakthrough at UK party level?
- In what ways are the Liberal Democrat policies to the left of Labour?

Comparative Electoral Success

In the 1960s, Labour saw itself as "the natural party of Government". Labour won the General Elections of 1964 and 1966. This was because it had captured the bulk of the (then) sizeable working class vote and a substantial section of the middle class. With Labour leading the "white hot heat of technology", the Conservatives were successfully portrayed as obsessed with class snobbery, as out of date and out of touch.

The Tories famously came back and Labour, until Tony Blair's re-invention of the party, spent many years in the wilderness. However, some commentators have suggested that Labour's recent successes, albeit with the assistance of the First Past The Post voting system (FPTP), has returned the party to its place as "the natural party of government".

In UK terms, Labour's successes in the 1997, 2001 and 2005 UK General Elections are staggering. These were three convincing victories. Labour won parliamentary majorities of 179 in 1997, 167 in 2001 and 66 in 2005. It won its "heartlands" and retained most of its "key marginals". However, Labour's success is rooted in the FPTP voting system. In none of these victories did the party win any more than 40% of the popular vote. In 2005, Labour won the General Election with just 35.2% of the popular vote.

Because of the demographic nature of constituency boundaries, it is estimated that for the Conservatives to achieve a General Election victory, the party will need a 10% lead over Labour in the polls. This is because the Conservatives tend to win their parliamentary seats with much larger majorities than Labour does. Because of the FPTP voting system, these huge majorities represent, in a sense, a waste of votes which would be better off, from a Conservative point of view, utilised in more marginal seats. So, unless David Cameron can persuade Conservative voters to move house into his party's target constituencies, it will be very difficult for the Conservatives to overturn Labour's in-built advantage.

Former First Minister Jack McConnell. The Labour Party in Scotland is not used to opposition.

However, a Conservative electoral victory is not impossible. Gordon Brown's famous decision to back down from a November 2007 General Election was due to a belief, confirmed by opinion poll evidence, that the Conservatives could win sufficient marginal seats to wipe out his Commons majority. Small wonder Labour has little time for voting reform.

In Scotland, until 2007, Labour has been no less dominant. Labour holds 41 of the 59 Scottish Westminster parliamentary seats. In both the 1999 and 2003 Scottish parliamentary elections Labour emerged as the largest party. Labour controlled 15 out of 32 Scottish local authorities and shared power in another four.

For the last fifty years, Labour has been Scotland's dominant political force. During the period of the 1980s, when Labour was out of contention for power at a UK level, the Labour Party in Scotland avoided the "loony" image it had acquired in England. "Scottish" Labour (Labour is a UK wide party but the party in Scotland increasingly emphasises its Scottish identity) held on to most of its UK parliamentary seats in Scotland. The Conservatives could not make a breakthrough. Labour was firmly in charge of most of Scotland's local authorities.

Scottish Labour can be seen as distinct from both old and new Labour. Scottish Labour introduced free personal care for the elderly and ruled out Foundation hospitals and selection for Scottish schools. Scottish Labour did not introduce "top-up fees" for university courses. Scottish Labour has had a much more fraternal relationship with trade unions and public sector workers than Tony Blair's government. Jack McConnell's Labour dominated Scottish Executive favoured "Scottish solutions for Scottish problems".

> Gordon Brown's famous decision to back down from a November 2007 General Election was due to a belief, confirmed by opinion poll evidence, that the Conservatives could win sufficient marginal seats to wipe out his Commons majority.

The loss of the 2007 Scottish Parliament elections to the SNP was a huge blow. Opposition has not come easy to a party used to government. Losing control of so many Scottish local authorities also hurt the party, but the introduction of the Single Transferable Vote (STV) made this almost inevitable.

However, despite forecasts of "wipe out", Scottish Labour gained 46 MSPs in the 2007 Scottish Parliament elections, only one less than the governing SNP. It has experienced and able politicians who will keep the new SNP Ministers on their toes. Labour won the most constituency seats in the 2007 Scottish Parliament elections.

The Liberal Democrats have to overcome the First Past the Post electoral system in order to have any meaningful chance of government. The party suffers from a widespread belief among many voters that a Liberal Democrat vote therefore is a "wasted vote", a view Labour and Conservative are content to encourage. The "wasted vote" argument thus becomes a self-fulfilling prophecy. Voters do not vote Liberal Democrat because they believe it to be a wasted vote. The Liberal Democrats do not win enough constituency seats because not enough voters vote for them! The Liberal Democrats regularly win around ¼ of the popular vote, yet win far fewer seats.

The party traditionally does well as a party of protest during by-elections and tends to hold constituency seats where it becomes established. In Scottish Parliament elections, the Scottish Liberal Democrats have more MSPs elected through the First Past the Post element of the Additional Member System than it has through the proportional list vote.

The SNP performs much better in elections to the Scottish Parliament than it does for Westminster elections. Voters appear to view the Westminster elections as an opportunity to elect a UK Government and form the view that the SNP is unlikely to do this, as it only stands candidates in Scotland's 59 Westminster constituencies. The SNP therefore has a credibility battle to overcome at Westminster which it has overcome in elections to the Scottish Parliament.

In 2007 the SNP became the most popular party in terms of votes cast and MSPs. It also became the largest party in Scottish local government. This was the first time Labour had come in second place in Scotland since 1959, when the Conservatives won more votes than Labour.

Activities

- Why did Labour see itself as the "natural" party of Government?
- Why has the First Past the Post voting system benefited Labour?
- Why were the Scottish Parliament elections not a complete disaster for Scottish Labour?
- Why might the SNP not do as well in Westminster elections as it does for Scottish Parliament elections?

2005 General Election

Labour won the 2005 General Election, but with a greatly reduced Commons majority with the lowest turnout since 1918. Labour lost 47 seats, giving the party a majority of 66. When taking turnout into account, Tony Blair's, and now Gordon Brown's Labour Party is governing with only 22% of the electorate having voted for them. Despite this, it was a historic win for Tony Blair. Labour has never before won three consecutive General Elections.

Labour's support for the war in Iraq led to a loss in support in 2005.

Labour suffered a 6% drop in the share of its vote. The Liberal Democrats were the main gainers but, once again, the First Past the Post electoral system deprived them of many seats it may have won under a different voting system. The Liberal Democrats won just short of 23% of the vote and won only 62 seats. This can be compared with Labour's 36% of the vote, gaining 355 seats, and the Conservatives' 198 seats from 33% of the popular vote.

Labour was on the defensive for most of the election campaign. The war in Iraq was a major issue. The Conservatives' support for the war blunted their attack. Conservative leader Michael Howard was only able to attack Tony Blair on his conduct and on his mistake in accepting advice that Saddam Hussein had weapons of mass destruction. Had the Conservatives opposed the war from the start, they would surely have been in a stronger position. Labour's fear was that its core vote would stay at home. This would allow the Conservatives to win the marginal seats Labour had campaigned so hard to win in 1997 and 2001.

Labour did lose votes among its core, working class (D, E) and lower middle class voters (C1), but not enough for the Conservatives to capitalise on. Labour successfully wooed so-called "school gate mum" voters. Support for Labour among women was 5% higher than among men. Opinion polls showed that Labour enjoyed support on issues such as the health service, child care and education, which female voters value.

The Liberal Democrats' opposition to university tuition fees was a popular policy with young voters.

The Liberal Democrats did well among young people. The Liberal Democrats' anti Iraq war stance and the party's opposition to university tuition fees clearly made the party popular among young people considering further or higher education. The Liberal Democrats gained 12 seats from Labour, including big gains in some student seats, including a 17% swing in Manchester Withington, a 15% swing in Cambridge, and a 14% swing in Hornsey and Wood Green. The Liberal Democrats will be hoping that these voters will stay with the party in the future. On the other hand, perhaps the potency of anti war and anti tuition fee feeling will have faded by the time the next General Election comes around.

And yet, many in the Liberal Democrats felt 2005 was to be their year. The party knew the voting system was against them. But a hung parliament was not an unrealistic target. Charles Kennedy would have been hoping to then enter into talks with Tony Blair on a "centre-left" coalition which could, in theory, have kept the Conservatives out of power forever. A centre left coalition would have led the Liberal Democrats to the holy grail of proportional representation, which would almost certainly boost

Liberal Democrat support even more and cement the party's position as a contender for power. Kennedy's leadership was strongly criticised by many within the party. They felt that he never showed the dynamism one would have expected of a young, popular Liberal Democrat leader on the cusp of an electoral breakthrough. The Liberal Democrats should have been the big winners, but they increased their share of the vote by only 3.7 percentage points.

The Conservatives in 2005 never managed to portray themselves as fit for government.

The Conservatives probably did not expect to overturn Tony Blair's majority in one fell swoop. Given the disasters of 1997 and 2001, internally the party will have been pleased that it turned the corner, in seats won, if not in overall public support. The Conservatives won an extra 33 seats and increased its support by just 1%. This was some way short of what was required for a Commons majority. But the party made inroads with the floating voters who had left the party for New Labour. The Conservatives also managed to prevent their core vote, among the elderly and the professional classes, from going over to the Liberal Democrats.

The Conservatives' campaign was criticised by some within the party as being too conservative. The Conservatives were clearly keen to shore up their support and this lack of cutting edge in campaigning perhaps meant that the party did not win as many seats as it could. The "are you thinking what we're thinking" bill boards only succeeded in attracting abusive responses, rather than setting the tone as previous Saatchi and Saatchi Conservative campaigns have.

While Michael Howard led from the front and was energetic in his attacks on Labour's record, too many voters agreed with Ann Widdicombe's famous opinion that there was "something of the night" about him. The Conservatives' replacement of Howard by the softer, more "metrosexual" David Cameron indicates that the party feels the leadership factor can make a significant difference to the mythical Worcester Woman the Tories need to win back.

In Scotland, Labour was dominant once again, winning 49 of the country's 56 seats. The Liberal Democrats did well in Scotland, gaining seats and finishing second overall.

2007 Scottish Elections

The 1990s saw the Conservatives in Scotland almost wiped out as a political force. Long-term cultural changes in Scottish societies, the closure of Scotland's traditional industries and personal animosity towards Margaret Thatcher all explain why the party, which once used to be Scotland's dominant political institution, became a fringe player. Scottish Labour became the establishment party. The SNP replaced the Conservative as Labour's rival. However, the SNP is also a social democratic party which shares the same broad brush social economic policies as Labour. Labour favours the Union with the UK, whereas the SNP's social democratic solutions focus on greater, and ultimately full, Scottish independence

Scottish Labour can rarely attack the SNP on ideological grounds. The SNP used to be portrayed by Labour as "Tartan Tories". However, with the SNP's opposition to Public Private Partnerships and the war in Iraq placing it to the left of Labour, this tactic would have been fruitless. Instead, Labour focused on the same kind of negative attacks the Conservatives in the UK used successfully against Old Labour.

Labour campaigned against the "recklessness" of "un-costed" nationalist policies. It used scare tactics to frighten voters against the "dangers" of separation. Note the language. At elections times Scottish Labour rarely mentions Scottish independence, but "separation". Most people associate independence with positive emotions. Who doesn't like to be independent? On the other hand, who likes separation?

However, it was the very negativity of Labour's 2007 campaign which appears to have been its downfall. A post-election study by academics from Strathclyde University found that: "The style of campaigning played a significant part in the outcome with the SNP's campaign perceived to be positive while Labour's was deemed negative. Although Alex Salmond may have contributed to the perception of the SNP as competent, there is no evidence that his lead over Jack McConnell in terms of personal popularity was a significant factor in the SNP's win."

In 2007 the SNP took over the government of Scotland in the Scottish Parliament. The SNP, for the first time, won the majority of Scottish seats and the majority of votes. They won seats in Labour "heartlands" such as Ayrshire, Dundee, Stirling, Falkirk and Edinburgh. The party also did well in the regional "list elections", at the expense of the Scottish Socialist Party/Solidarity and the Scottish Greens.

The 2007 Scottish Parliament election became a two horse race between the SNP and Scottish Labour. As John Curtice points out "It may well be that the close contest between the SNP and Labour meant that fewer voters were willing to express sympathy for the Greens by giving them their regional vote – as they appeared to do in 2003"

The SNP are now the largest party in 10 Scottish local authorities. In addition, Aberdeen, Argyll and Bute, East Lothian, Edinburgh, Highland,

Renfrewshire, West Dunbartonshire and West Lothian all have SNP councillors in a ruling coalition. Only Glasgow and North Lanarkshire have Labour-controlled local authorities. In councils such as Edinburgh and West Lothian, coalitions have been formed to exclude Labour. It seems that after years of Labour rule, other parties are now ganging up on Labour. On the other hand, in East Dunbartonshire, Labour and the Tories have formed a coalition to keep out the SNP!

> Given the party's profile as a partner in Scottish government and the party's popular anti-war stance, the Scottish Liberal Democrats should really have been expected to increase their number of MSPs. Instead, for the first time since 1970, the party lost constituencies.

While the Conservatives opposed the setting up of the Scottish Parliament, devolution, or rather the Additional Member System (AMS), has been the party's lifeline in Scotland. At the 2007 Scottish elections, the Conservatives gained a total of eighteen MSPs. Only four of them have been elected by the traditional First Past the Post element of the system.

Realistically, the Scottish Conservatives knew they would not win power at the 2007 Scottish Parliament elections. They would though dearly love to become serious contenders, at least to become coalition partners. Annabel Goldie will have been disappointed at only achieving 14% of the Scottish vote. The Scottish Conservatives have "bottomed out" at this figure for some years now. The party shows few signs of raising its popularity much above this figure.

Annabel Goldie however, is proving to be a strong leader and a popular character in Scottish politics. Even if the Scottish Tories have declined from their dominance in the 1950s, they have, at least, returned to some kind of political respectability.

The Scottish Liberal Democrats will have been disappointed in their performance at the 2007 Scottish Parliament elections. The Scottish Liberal Democrats did well at the 2005 General Election, coming second to Labour. The party also achieved a famous by-election win in Dunfermline West, Prime Minister Gordon Brown's home turf, when Willie Rennie won what should have been a safe Labour seat. Given the party's profile as a partner in Scottish government and the party's popular anti-war stance, the Scottish Liberal Democrats should really have been expected to increase their number of MSPs. Instead, for the first time since 1970, the party lost constituencies.

In winning only 16 seats, they are, once again, Scotland's 4th party. Moreover, they are now out of power and on the back benches. Nicol Stephen rejected Alex Salmond's offer of talks over a coalition. Stephen refused to even talk to Salmond unless the SNP abandoned its plan to hold a referendum on independence. On the face of it, the Scottish Liberal Democrats have at least as much in common with the SNP as they have with Scottish Labour. Both parties oppose the Council Tax. Both parties are in favour of reviewing the Scottish Parliament's powers. Both parties are in favour of left of centre education, health and criminal justice policies.

Presumably the Scottish Liberal Democrats prefer a period of opposition in which it can try to reassert its own identity and its unique selling point to Scottish voters. Perhaps the Scottish Liberal Democrats do not want to be seen as a party that will go into government with just anyone. On the other hand, some Scottish Liberal Democrat supporters believe this is what being liberal and democratic is all about: being prepared to listen to other parties' policies on their merits, rather than their party label.

Activities

Evaluate the strengths and weaknesses of the four major parties' campaigns in the 2005 UK and 2007 Scottish elections.

You should focus on

- Party policies
- Leadership style
- Campaign strategies
- Election results

T h e   B i g   P i c t u r e

There are now four electoral systems being used in the UK.

- UK General elections – First Past the Post (FPTP)
- Scottish Parliament elections – The Additional Member System (AMS)
- Scottish local government, Northern Ireland Assembly elections – Single Transferable vote (STV)
- European elections – The Party List (Northern Ireland uses the STV for European elections too)

Why, you may ask, do we have so many different voting systems? Why can't we use the same voting system for all four elections? There are two parts to the answer. The first takes us back to a famous phrase by the Russian leader Joseph Stalin. "It is not who wins the most votes that matters. It is who counts the votes".

No-one would accuse UK governments of actual electoral fraud, although there was plenty of incompetence during the counting of the 2007 Scottish elections. Joseph Stalin's point, however cynical, has a resonance because the type of electoral system which is chosen has a big impact on the electoral result. All the political parties know this. Their support for an electoral system will have as much to do with their own self interest as with theoretical arguments over "fairness" or "democracy".

For example, the Labour Party is in favour of the

First Past the Post (FPTP) system. FPTP suits Labour. Labour won the 2005 General Election, and the right to run the country for up to five years, with a popular vote of just 35% and a turnout of just 61%. A switch to a proportional representation system (PR) system, such as STV, would severely threaten Labour's chances of winning power. It would take a very magnanimous Labour leader to support a move away from FPTP. The phrase, "turkeys voting for Christmas," comes to mind.

Likewise in Northern Ireland, the STV system is used. But this is deployed for a higher set of political principles. Given voting loyalties in Northern Ireland, a FPTP voting system would, in all likelihood, result in a win for the Democratic Unionist Party (DUP) with its traditional antagonist Sinn Fein (SF) in Opposition.

Such a polarised result would increase political tensions in an already divided society where peace is a greater prize than party political advantage. Given the same voting intentions, an STV Northern Ireland assembly election would be likely to create a DUP/SF coalition. Such was the result of the 2007 Northern Ireland Assembly elections. Peace in Northern Ireland is more secure, partly because of STV.

Secondly, there is no perfect electoral system. Each supporter of majoritarian systems (such as FPTP), proportional (STV) or hybrid (AMS) has convincing arguments of its fairness and practicality. The debate over the "fairness" of FPTP is now a real issue in UK politics. In the 2005 General Election, if seats had been distributed purely in proportion to votes won, the result might have been very different.

Seats won by	FPTP	PR
Labour	356	239
Conservative	197	209
Liberal Democrat	62	142
SNP	6	11
Others	25	45

This is purely hypothetical, and voters may well have voted differently if there was a PR system in place, but the figures do point to an "unfairness" of the current system.

Unless the Labour Party completely implodes, Tony Blair and his successor, Gordon Brown have a mandate to run the country, with a majority of just 66 MPs, on their own, for five years, with just 35.2% of the popular vote. This is the lowest share of the vote any Government has achieved since the Reform Act of 1832. A PR system would surely have resulted in a Labour/Liberal Democrat coalition. The Independent newspaper was so outraged that it organised an online petition to 10 Downing Street.

The social science of "psephology" is devoted to the analysis of voting behaviour. Academics, such as John Curtice of Strathclyde University, are regularly invited to television election specials to explain why voters voted for a particular party. Voting is a complex matter. Modern society is complex. There is no one single reason which can explain why a party won a particular election. In UK General Elections, there are 646 constituency elections going on simultaneously, from John O'Groats to Lands End.

Amongst these geographical extremities are voters from diverse social/economic and ethnic backgrounds. Some are rich, some are poor. Some are professionals from parents of professional backgrounds. Some are "first generation" middle class, whose parents come from working class backgrounds. Some voters are strongly religious. Some are not. Some read "quality newspapers", some read the "red tops" or no newspapers at all.

An increasing number of voters get all their political information online. In some constituencies, the so-called "marginal" constituencies, voters will be wooed by high profile politicians and subjected to

political campaigns of military precision. Others, who live in so-called safe seats, are unlikely to be given anything like the same attention from political parties.

It is, therefore, important not to make crude generalisations about why people vote the way they do. There is a variety of influences, several of which overlap.

So, if we understand from the beginning that this is a complex issue and that there are many influences on voters, we are off to a good start. It is important to critically assess the key long-term influences on voters such as social class, gender, ethnicity, age and religion along with shorter-term influences, such as the impact of party leaders, the party campaign and controversial issues which come alive both during and in the lead up to elections.

Chapter 9
The Electoral Systems Debate

The debate over electoral systems can be complex, with many nuances and grey areas. As such, misunderstandings are commonplace. Some voters believe "PR" is a voting system in itself. It is not. There are many different PR voting systems. STV is one and there are various forms of STV! FPTP is not a PR system! The AMS, in truth, is a hybrid of both majoritarian FPTP and the PR STV. But, for purposes of convenience, we shall treat AMS as a PR system, although, as PR campaigners would testify, the AMS is not a pure PR system.

Some voters believe that "PR" systems lead to confusion. There was confusion over the counting of votes in the 2007 Scottish elections. However, there were fewer spoiled ballot papers in the PR STV local government election than in the hybrid AMS elections to the Scottish Parliament. The fact that the

Voting is a complex matter. Modern society is complex. There is no one single reason which can explain why a party won a particular election.

95

Scotland Office placed the two ballot papers for the Scottish Parliament elections on one ballot paper must have contributed to the confusion. Crafty, yet wholly legitimate, tactics by the SNP in inserting "Alex Salmond for First Minister", rather than the names of the party's list candidates, may not have helped either.

Voting in a STV election is remarkably simple. The voter simply ranks candidates in order of preference. The mathematics of working out the eventual winners is complicated. But this is outwith the scope of political analysis. As the saying goes, cars are complicated; but you do not need to know how a car works in order to drive one.

Some voters also draw the mistaken conclusion that "PR leads to unstable government". It can, and sometimes does, but not always! FPTP can lead to instability too. Whether a government is stable or not does not depend exclusively on its electoral system. For example, the Labour/Liberal Democrat coalition, which was in control of the Scottish Parliament from 1999-2007, was far from unstable. It legislated on divisive and controversial issues, from introducing STV to local government elections to university tuition fees. It did so through negotiation and compromise. Indeed, the complaint from the opposition parties was that the two parties were too cosy with each other!

Another misunderstanding is that "FPTP provides strong government". FPTP usually does provide strong government. For example, the Conservatives were in complete power in the UK for 18 years, winning four consecutive General Elections, despite never gaining any more than 44% of the popular vote. The UK usually does just have one party in power, governing on its own for a full parliamentary term. This has been the case in each General Election since 1979.

But, coalitions happen under FPTP too. Britain was forced to have two General Elections in 1974 because the first, in February 1974, resulted in a minority Labour Government which did not have an overall majority of MPs in the House of Commons. The second election, in October 1974, provided Labour with a slim majority, but the Labour Government eventually had to form a formal coalition with the Liberals in 1977.

Likewise, the last year of John Major's Conservative

Government in 1996-97 witnessed an informal deal done between the minority Conservative Government and the Ulster Unionists. A "gentleman's agreement" was reached whereby the Ulster Unionists would votes with the Conservatives in order to keep Prime Minister John Major in power.

> **Activities**
>
> * Why would some political parties like to see FPTP replaced with a more proportional voting system?
> * Why is it inaccurate to say that "PR" leads to confusion?
> * What evidence is there that FPTP does not always lead to strong government?

First Past the Post (FPTP)

UK General Elections are fought under FPTP. The country is divided into 646 constituencies, usually referred to as "seats". A candidate wins a seat by gaining more votes than any other candidate. The party which wins the most seats goes on to form the Government. It is fairly straightforward and its supporters argue that its beauty lies in its simplicity.

There are other, more important arguments in favour of FPTP.

FPTP usually produces a decisive result

The key word here is *usually*. The last seven General Elections: 1979, 1983, 1987, 1992, 1997, 2001 and 2005, have each produced a decisive result: One party gained a majority of MPs over all the others in the House of Commons.

Because UK MPs are usually loyal to their political leadership, and the parliamentary whip system tends to ensure this party discipline, the Government can pass the legislation it desires. The Government can claim it has the voters' support to deliver such legislation.

This notion of a *mandate* from the voters is critical for supporters of FPTP. During the General Election campaign, the parties present to the voters their manifesto. The party manifesto contains flagship policies which would be made into law should the party win power. As FPTP elections usually deliver a decisive result, the governing party tens to have a five --year term to fulfil the promises it made to the voters. If the Government does not deliver on its promises, the Government has no-one else to blame – it had the majority in the House of Commons to do so.

FPTP is very efficient at removing Governments which do not deliver their promises. The Conservatives, who had been dominant throughout the 1980s and most of the 1990s, were swept from office by Labour in 1997. The country wanted political change and FPTP enabled it to happen.

FPTP usually delivers stable Government

Here in the UK we are used to stable Government. General Elections or major changes in Government are few and far between. We know who the Government will be over a four/five year term.

Michelle Mone is the founder and co-owner of MJM International, a multi-million pound lingerie company. Global businesses like economic stability. Supporters of FPTP claim FPTP provides more stable government than a PR system does.

Business, especially global business, does not like instability. Who wants to invest in a country where there is instability over key economic issues such as taxation, interest and currency rates? Supporters of FPTP claim that FPTP creates stable government and therefore stable economic conditions. It is claimed that the quality of life this stability brings to the UK outweighs complaints over the alleged "mathematical unfairness" of the system.

FPTP allows by-elections to register protest

There are usually by-elections in a FPTP voting system. These happen when an MP retires or dies. They can be used by the voters to show their disapproval of a Government which has strayed from its manifesto commitments or taken unpopular decisions.

The Dunfermline West by-election of February 2006, following the death of Labour MP Rachel Squires, is a good example. Dunfermline West is the neighbouring constituency to Prime Minister Gordon Brown's. The Labour Government however had become unpopular, even in its heartland of West Fife. Opinion polls had shown that voters were unhappy with Tony Blair's leadership, the war in Iraq and a suspicion of political "cronyism". The allegations over "Cash for Honours" (ultimately unfounded) had a high profile during the election campaign. Voters in Dunfermline West took the opportunity to protest against the Labour Party. The Liberal Democrat candidate Willie Rennie won.

Supporters of FPTP argue that this is democracy in action. If we had an AMS, and the MP elected had come from the party list, there would have been no vehicle for the voters to express their dissatisfaction. Labour would simply have replaced one representative with another.

FPTP disadvantages

Not everyone agrees with the FPTP electoral system. FPTP was dominant in the UK for most of the 20th century, but the tide appears to be turning against it. Critics have several arguments against it.

Is stable government good government?

Critics of FPTP accept that FPTP usually delivers stable government. But, they question whether stable government is always good government? Is it not better to have a coalition partner, offering another point of view, which will provide the country with better government? PR supporters claim that the longer a party is in power on its own, the more likely it is to become removed from the political mood of the nation. Margaret Thatcher's Conservatives came up with the Poll Tax, a policy so unpopular it led to rioting in the streets and her eventual downfall as Prime Minister.

Likewise, in 2005, Liberal Democrat leader Charles Kennedy was opposed to the war in Iraq. A STV-run UK General Election would have been likely to create a "hung parliament" and deprive Labour of absolute power. This may have meant a coalition between Labour and the Liberal Democrats, the price of which may have been the end of British support for the war in Iraq.

FPTP doesn't always produce decisive results

A hung parliament is when one party has the most seats, but if the opposition parties join together, they can out-vote the Government. The current SNP-led Scottish Parliament, elected by AMS, has a hung parliament. Hung parliaments happen under FPTP too.

In 1977-79, Labour had to go into coalition with the Liberal Party. In 1996-97, John Major's Conservatives went into an informal coalition with the Ulster Unionist Party. Was it democratic that the Ulster Unionists who, after all, only represent constituencies in Northern Ireland, should have such a big say in the running of the country?

Does FPTP deliver a fair result?

The 2005 General Election was described by the Independent newspaper as THE most unfair election result of all time. Labour is able to run the country, on its own, for five years on the basis of 35.2% of the votes cast. The Liberal Democrats won 22% of the votes but only 10% of the seats. It is argued that such a result is undemocratic. It is claimed that Tony Blair's Government, elected by a minority of all voters (and less than 2/3 of eligible voters bothered to vote) had no mandate for its election promises.

FPTP creates voter apathy

FPTP is based on candidates winning individual constituencies. Parties with a social class base in constituencies have an inbuilt advantage. Voters of similar social classes tend to live next to one another. Labour, for example, has its "core" supporters within predominantly working class constituencies.

The seat of Coatbridge, Chryston and Bellshill is the safest seat in the UK. In 2005, its MP, Labour's Tom Clarke, won the seat with a majority of 19, 519 votes over the second-placed SNP candidate. The Conservative candidate, Lindsay Paterson, won just 2,775 votes.

Given this reality, at the next General Election, what motivation is there for a Conservative minded voter to turn out? It is highly likely that the Labour candidate, whoever it may be, will win. The fact that just 57% of voters in Coatbridge, Chryston and Bellshill bothered to vote is further evidence for anti-FPTP campaigners. In such safe seats, there is little motivation for voters to vote.

The influence of social class on UK elections, combined with the FPTP system, means that General Elections are won and lost in the marginal seats where the winning majority is low and the election result is in doubt. Political parties target these seats and de-prioritise their safe seats. Instead of having large numbers of loyal voters, marginal seats have more floating voters.

During the course of an election campaign, floating voters may change their minds. It is argued therefore, that the FPTP system creates two classes of voter: the 100,000 or so voters who live in marginal seats, and the rest.

Political parties pay attention to voters in marginal seats. On the other hand, voters in the safe seats can, to a large degree, be taken for granted, thus their views become less sought-after.

New developments in FPTP

While FPTP produces majority governments, it does not always deliver decisive results. The Labour Government, elected in 2005, had on paper a majority of 66 over all the other parties. In March 2006, Tony Blair needed the votes of Conservative MPs to have his Education Bill passed in the House of Commons. So much for FPTP producing a decisive result.

The Conservatives, who used to do well from FPTP, no longer do well from it. Labour benefits from FPTP. But the Conservatives do not.

At the 2005 General Election, the Conservatives did almost as well as Labour, winning 32.3% of the vote. But the Conservatives gained fewer seats. This is because of demographic changes and constituency boundary arrangements. Safe Labour constituencies tend to be smaller and have smaller majorities. The Conservatives, on the other hand are more likely to win their safe seats, which have more voters living in them, with bigger majorities. These large majorities amount to wasted votes. For party strategists, winning seats by majorities of 15,000 is inefficient. It would be better to have these winning votes spread around a little bit more.

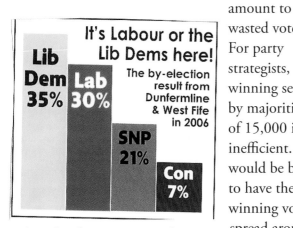

The Liberal Democrats are becoming more sophisticated in FPTP elections.

FPTP is now making it harder for the Conservatives to translate their votes into seats. It is estimated that, for the Conservatives to win a UK General Election, the party will need to have a 10% lead over Labour in order to overcome the demographic advantage the current FPTP system gives Labour.

The Liberal Democrats are becoming more

sophisticated in FPTP elections. They have always been against FPTP. They have however adjusted their campaigning techniques to the realities of FPTP. The Liberal Democrats lie in second place in most seats in England. Where the Liberal Democrats have won seats, sometimes it is by clever use of tactical voting. Why, in a Conservative marginal seat, with the Liberal Democrats in close second place and Labour a distant third, would a Labour voter vote Labour? Surely this would amount to a wasted vote.

Would it not suit the Labour cause better to vote for the Liberal Democrat candidate, whose policies are closer to Labour, and who has a realistic chance of winning? Such is the logic of many Liberal Democrat campaigns which cleverly emphasise their "winnability" to well informed voters. The Liberal Democrats' political opponents are incensed by this tactic and claim the "Fib-Dems" exaggerate their support to encourage tactical voting.

Activities

- What is meant by a "mandate"?
- Why is "economic stability" such a strong argument for FPTP?
- What part do by-elections play in the UK system of government?
- Why do some people believe FPTP is a very unfair electoral system?
- Why might PR create voter apathy?
- Why might FPTP create two classes of voter?
- Why does FPTP favour the Labour Party more than

a) the Liberal Democrats?
b) the Conservative Party?

- How have the Liberal Democrats used tactical voting to overcome the disadvantages of FPTP?
-
- Why have the Liberal Democrats been branded the "Fib-Dems" by their political opponents?
-
- Draw a large spider diagram of the key arguments for and against FPTP. Give examples for each point on the diagram.

Interview with Willie Rennie MP

Modernity: What is your preferred voting system?

Willie Rennie: As you're probably aware, it has been a long-standing policy of the Liberal Democrats that we want to see proportional representation used as the voting system in this country. This year's Scottish elections proved that the system works, and the problems encountered were not as a result of the system itself. With PR, the proportion of MPs elected for each party is roughly equal to the proportion of votes that party received in the election. In Parliament, if 22% of the country voted Lib Dem, as they did in 2005, we would get about 142 MPs, instead of the 62 we actually got.

Modernity: Why do you believe this is more democratic than the others?

Willie Rennie: With PR nearly every vote counts. And on average across the whole globe, turnout in 'first past the post' elections is 58%, similar to this country, while turnout in proportional systems is 68%. PR kills two birds with one stone; more people vote, and more of those votes count.

Modernity: How have the Liberal Democrats campaigned in First Past the Post elections which, on the whole, do not favour your party?

Willie Rennie: We focus on trying to engage as many people as possible, whether that is through focus

leaflets or canvassing, we believe it is important to keep the electorate interested and informed. The method has served us pretty well in the past, given the inherent disadvantage of being the third party in a FPTP system. Like other parties, we also have a list of most winnable seats where most of our effort is focussed.

Modernity: What were the secret(s) of your by-election success?

Willie Rennie: As mentioned in the previous answer it was all about engaging people, we had a huge amount of help from local activists which was a big factor. I also think that people were tired of the same old Labour that they'd been experiencing over many years, and were looking for an alternative. That said, I also believe that the Lib Dems in Scotland were performing well in government and the result in Dunfermline and West Fife was partially an acknowledgement of this.

Modernity: Do you believe the voting system for Westminster will be changed in the foreseeable future?

Willie Rennie: I certainly hope so. As we see it, bringing in PR will improve and strengthen the UK's democratic systems. I'm not so sure the other parties would be so keen; the current system works heavily in their favour.

Modernity: What impact do you think the media has on voters?

Willie Rennie: It varies. The media performs a vital

role in informing the public, whether it is through 'old' media such as newspapers, or through 'new' media like websites and the like. I think the internet has had a positive impact on politics, making it more accessible, you only have to look at the debates the Democrats in the USA held that were broadcast on You Tube for evidence of this. However the media can also sometimes have a negative impact; if they make their mind up about something, it can be difficult to change. I also think the way the media works makes it difficult for a third party to get the publicity we deserve.

Modernity: Do you identify "core" Liberal Democrat voters? If so, what makes these voters different from "floating" voters?

Willie Rennie: We do, I think the difference is fairly self explanatory; they believe in the very core values of the party and have done for some time. There are increasing numbers of people who are breaking free from traditional party allegiances, which is a huge opportunity for the Liberal Democrats.

Modernity: What can the Liberal Democrats do to carve out a unique identity in an increasingly crowded political centre ground?

Willie Rennie: It is probably rather simplistic to view the centre ground as a homogeneous mass, when the reality is that it is a complex group of individuals who have a wide and varied set of interests. Different people vote in different ways for different reasons. By using modern campaign techniques, it is possible to appeal to these individuals in a targeted way to promote our policies and values. Our traditional values of community, freedom, openness, equality and opportunity appeal to large sections of the population.

No matter how hard the other parties try to shed their ties to the trade unions and big business, their beliefs and policies are undeniably affected by these links which makes it extremely difficult for them to genuinely appeal to that centre ground. Our freedom from these vested interests enables us to base our policies on our values.

For example, we have developed effective policies on the environment by proposing to shift taxation from income to pollution. We are also defending civil liberties by opposing the introduction of ID cards and promoting international relations through dialogue and understanding rather than relying on military means.

The Additional Member System (AMS)

The AMS is used for elections to the Scottish Parliament. The AMS was introduced as a result of negotiations between the organisations which designed the blueprint for the Scottish Parliament. This body was known as the Scottish Constitutional Convention (SCC).

The Scottish Labour Party, the largest party in the SCC, would have preferred a traditional FPTP system. FPTP benefits Scottish Labour, with its strong, class-based, geographical core vote. The Scottish Liberal Democrats would have preferred the STV. A PR system would be of greater benefit to the Scottish Liberal Democrats, with its voters dispersed around the country. Both the Scottish Conservatives and SNP boycotted the SCC and did not have a strong input into decision making on the AMS, which has now been used three times for Scottish Parliament elections.

The AMS is a hybrid system. It contains both a FPTP element and a PR element. 73 of the Scottish Parliament's MSPs are elected by FPTP. These are constituency MSPs, elected in exactly the same way as voters elect constituency MPs for Westminster elections. In fact, the exact same constituency boundaries are used for both Scottish Parliament and Westminster elections. The remaining 56 MSPs are elected through the proportional element of the AMS.

The SCC sought a different kind of politics from that which exists at Westminster. It believed that an AMS would allow minority parties greater chance of representation. The AMS, it was argued, would also be less likely to enable any one party to dominate the Scottish Parliament, in the way both Conservative and Labour have at Westminster. The SCC believed AMS would force parties to be less confrontational. They would have to discuss and negotiate legislation with each other. So it has proved. The first two elections to the Scottish Parliament, in 1999 and 2003, resulted in coalition government between Scottish Labour and the Scottish Liberal Democrats. The 2007 Scottish elections delivered a minority SNP Scottish Government.

Voting for the AMS is uncomplicated. The voter

votes twice, placing an "X" each time. The first vote is for a constituency Member of the Scottish Parliament (MSP).The second vote is for an "additional member", usually described as a "regional list" MSP.

For example, in Dumfries in the 2007 Scottish Parliament election, the Scottish Labour candidate, Elaine Murray, won more votes than any of her rivals and became the constituency MSP for Dumfries. However, under the AMS, Dumfries is part of the wider, regional constituency of South of Scotland. There are, in total, eight wider regional constituencies across Scotland and each has seven additional list members allocated to it. The AMS attempts to compensate voters of parties who may have secured a number of votes spread out across the wider regional constituency, but not concentrated in any one smaller constituency. List seats are allocated according to the proportion of the vote each party receives, hence the name, the Additional Member System.

Elaine Murray MSP, Dumfries.

The end result of the election in Dumfries is that while Elaine Murray is the constituency MSP, there are 7 additional MSPs for the South of Scotland region.

So, for example, if a constituent in Dumfries has an issue in the area that needs the MSP's attention e.g. crime, he/she could approach Elaine Murray, the constituency MSP, to resolve the matter. But he/she could, approach a "list" MSP instead, such as the SNP's Alasdair Morgan, who is one of the list MSPs for South of Scotland.

The AMS gives smaller parties a chance

Not all voters in Scotland support the established parties. Because of the AMS, supporters of smaller parties such as the Scottish Green Party can vote, knowing that their vote will not be "wasted". Thanks to the proportional element of the AMS, their party will have a realistic chance of gaining some representation.

Scottish Green MSPs, such as Robin Harper, have made a strong contribution to the work of the Scottish Parliament. The Scottish Greens, who used to be a fringe party, have now become a genuine political force.

Likewise, the Scottish Socialist Party (SSP), until its implosion in 2006, represented the views of voters in Scotland who sought more radical socialist changes to Scottish society. The AMS allowed the SSP to gain seven MSPs in 2003 and to propose bills on issues such as free schools meals for all pupils in Scottish schools, as well as voice opposition to the war in Iraq.

The AMS means that it is unlikely any one party will have complete control. Power, as Lord Acton famously said, tends to corrupt. Absolute power absolutely corrupts. Because FPTP usually hands one party a monopoly of political power, supporters of AMS argue that better decision making can be made when parties are forced to discuss and negotiate legislation with one another, rather than bulldoze legislation against a numerically weaker opposition.

AMS usually leads to coalition government, and in the first two elections to the Scottish Parliament this has happened (although not, of course, the 2007 Scottish Parliament election). This, it is argued, is a good thing. The compromise over tuition fees, with repayment of fees postponed until after the student has gained a job with a professional salary is seen as an honourable and sensible policy reached after compromise and negotiation between two partners in government.

AMS disadvantages

The AMS, however, has been controversial. For example, in East Kilbride, Labour's Andy Kerr is the constituency MSP. In the 2007 Scottish Parliament election, he defeated the SNP's candidate, Linda Fabiani, by 1,972 votes. But, Linda Fabiani stood as a candidate in the regional list election and, despite being "rejected" by the voters of East Kilbride, Linda Fabiani was returned as an MSP.

Not only this, as a result of the SNP winning control of the Scottish Government, Linda Fabiani was appointed to the Cabinet post of Minister for Europe, External Affairs and Culture. Who is the "real" MSP for East Kilbride? Is there a "real" MSP, or are all MSPs, both constituency and list, of equal status? Former Labour MP Brian Wilson (in) famously dismissed list MSPs as "a waste of space".

The AMS delivers unelected MSPs

In August 2007, only four months after being elected as a List MSP for Lothians, SNP MSP Stefan Tymkewycz resigned from the Scottish Parliament. As well as being an MSP, Stefan Tymkewycz was also an elected Councillor in City of Edinburgh Council. He felt that it was not possible for him to do the two jobs properly.

> Margo MacDonald is a well-known and popular personality in Edinburgh. Had she been a "normal" candidate, without a media profile, the party machine would surely have kept her out of politics.

However, there is no facility in the Scottish Parliament's AMS for an election to replace him. The SNP duly selected Shirley-Anne Somerville, a press officer with the Royal College of Nursing, as an MSP. Shirley-Anne Somerville was next on the SNP Lothians List. No member of the public (outside of SNP party members) had a say in who one of their MSPs should be. Is this fair?

Are parties more powerful than voters?

In some parties, a high position on the party list is more important than connecting with voters. Most of the Conservative and SNP MSPs are regional list MSPs. To become an MSP for these parties, it is in a sense more important to be popular with small groups of party activists than it is to communicate with the voters. Gaining 1st or 2nd place on the Conservative or SNP party list will mean a good chance of election to the Scottish Parliament. There is no requirement for political parties to name their regional list candidates.

Margo MacDonald MSP, Lothians

The voter need never even know the candidate's name.

This explains why, in 2003, Margo MacDonald, an experienced and popular MSP, resigned from the SNP and ran as an Independent candidate. As a result of internal SNP rivalry, Margo MacDonald was placed a lowly 6th on the SNP's list for the Lothians region. This meant that, if she did not leave the SNP and run as an Independent, she would have had no realistic prospect of being elected. She decided to stand for election as an Independent candidate, and won.

This, however, is the exception rather than the rule. Margo MacDonald is a well-known and popular personality in Edinburgh. Had she been a "normal" candidate, without a media profile, the party machine would surely have kept her out of politics.

A solution to this problem would be to allow voters to rank prospective regional list MSPs in some kind of order. But this is really how the STV system works. So, why not abolish the AMS and replace it

with a STV system?
A government no-one voted for?

It is argued that under FPTP, voters have a clear choice. If your favourite party wins and forms the Government, it has a five year opportunity to fulfil its election pledges.

It may, as was the case with Labour in 2005, be elected by only 35% of the voters, but Labour did win more seats than any other party.

In an AMS coalition, it is possible to have a "partnership", or coalition, that was not presented to the voters as an option. It may even include parties whose policies were not particularly popular with the voters. For example, the Scottish Liberal Democrats finished a distant fourth in the 1999 and 2003 Scottish Parliament elections. On both occasions the Scottish Liberal Democrats became partners in Government. But the Scottish Labour-Liberal Democrat Partnership Agreement was never presented to the electorate. No-one, as they say, votes for a coalition. Instead, legislation arrives as the result of negotiation and compromise in "smoke filled rooms".

If the AMS is more democratic than FPTP, surely it should have been the second most popular party, the SNP, who was invited to join the coalition? So much for a "new kind of politics"! Labour and the SNP are bitter rivals. Labour and the Liberal Democrats had much more in common and were much more likely to reach agreement on issues.

At the 2003 Scottish Parliament elections, the

combined total of Labour/Liberal Democrat votes amounted to 41% of the overall vote. The Government still represented the wishes of a minority of voters. Not that much different from the much criticised FPTP.

The Single Transferable Vote (STV)

The STV is used for Scottish local authority elections and in Northern Ireland Assembly elections. In an STV election, the parties can stand more than one candidate and voters have more than one vote. They rank candidates in order of preference, putting a "1" for their favourite and so on, depending on how many candidates there are.

Constituencies are larger and voters have more than one elected representative. In order to be elected, candidates need to reach a "quota". Under STV, seats are allocated according to a formula.

The quota =
number of votes cast +1, divided by the number of votes in the constituency.

STV was introduced to Scottish local government elections as part of the 2003 Partnership agreement between Scottish Labour and the Scottish Liberal Democrats. Scottish Labour did not wish to see STV introduced, as it knew it would lose many of its elected councillors. However, it was the price paid for Scottish Liberal Democrat support in the 2003-07 Scottish Parliament coalition. Scottish Labour expected to lose many of its councillors in these elections, and so it proved.

STV and Scottish local government elections

STV has transformed the political complexion of Scotland's 32 local authorities. FPTP was of

Activities

- Why is the AMS not a "pure" PR system?
- Why did the Scottish Constitutional Convention (SCC) decide on an AMS for Scottish Parliament elections?
- What is the main difference between a constituency MSP and a list MSP?
- Try to find out the names of your constituency MSP and your seven additional "list" MSPs.
- Why might the AMS be good for parties such as the Scottish Green Party?
- Why might coalition government be a good thing?
- Why might the AMS cause confusion among voters as to who their MSP is?
- Why can the AMS be said to create "unelected" MSPs?
- To what extent can the AMS make political parties more powerful than the voters?
- Why might the AMS be criticised as undemocratic?
- Draw a large spider diagram of the key arguments for and against the AMS. Give examples for each point on the diagram.

Glasgow City Council remains Labour controlled. But, Labour in Glasgow now faces a strong opposition. Throughout the country, the SNP became the largest party in Scottish local government.

great advantage to the Labour Party. In the 1999 Midlothian local authority elections, Labour won 46% of the vote but 94% of the seats! Under STV, Labour, which used to govern many local authorities single-handedly, is now in second place to the SNP, in terms of both votes and elected councillors. Only Glasgow and North Lanarkshire have Labour controlled local authorities.

As expected, the STV has delivered coalition government. 21 local authorities have multi-party coalitions forming governing administrations. Parties, which used to be sworn enemies, have had to find common ground with one another.

There are only 5 councils with single-party majority administrations. These councils are Eilean Siar (Ind), Glasgow City (Labour), North Lanarkshire (Labour), Orkney Islands (Ind) and Shetland Islands (Ind). In addition there are six local authorities with single-party 'minority' administrations. These are: Clackmannanshire (Labour), East Ayrshire (SNP), Inverclyde (Labour), Midlothian (Labour), North Ayrshire (Labour) and, South Ayrshire (Conservative).

While the process of forming coalitions took time, all of Scotland's 32 local authorities now have a governing administration in place. In local authorities such as City of Edinburgh and West Lothian, coalitions have been formed to exclude Scottish Labour. It seems that after years of Labour rule, other parties have now ganged up on Labour.

On the other hand, in East Dunbartonshire, Scottish

Labour and the Scottish Conservatives have formed a coalition to keep the SNP out! Supporters of STV argue that the PR voting system has a number of distinct advantages over both FPTP and AMS.

STV allows voters to choose within parties

The added value of STV is that it allows voters to choose within as well as between parties. For example, under FPTP, if a voter wishes to vote Labour, there is only one Labour candidate for the voter to choose. If the voter does not like the nominated Labour candidate, the voter will have the choice of voting for that candidate or not voting at all.

However, under STV, the political parties will, more often than not, nominate more than one candidate for election. This gives the voter more choice. It also keeps elected politicians on their toes. There are no more "safe seats", where established politicians can almost rely on being re-elected due to the party label. A voter can vote for a different representative within that party.

In STV all votes count

Just like the AMS, all votes are tallied up and reallocated. In STV, the voter ranks candidates in order of preference. A voter does not have to use all the votes he/she has. The voter can rank in order of preference, but if there is only one candidate he/she wishes to vote for, he/she simply puts a "1" beside that name and walks away. Simple!

105

STV gives smaller parties a greater chance

Like the AMS, the STV gives smaller parties a better chance of getting elected. All across Scotland in 2007, Scottish Green Party candidates and Independent candidates were elected to Scotland's local authorities. The SNP broke Labour's long-held dominance of Scottish local government.

In many cases a new breed of politicians was elected. Aberdeen City Council has several youthful SNP councillors. Callum McCaig was elected at the age of 22. Councillor Mark McDonald was just 26 when elected. At the age of 21, Kirsty West is Aberdeen City Council's education spokesperson. Her younger brother John, who was 18 when he was elected, became Aberdeen's youngest ever Deputy Lord Provost. He is responsible for chairing full council meetings, at which multi-million pound decisions affecting Aberdeen will be made.

STV has its critics. Since STV was used in local government elections, these criticisms are not just abstract, but are now based on real political experience.

Multi members confuse voters. Some critics have raised the issue of "where does the buck stop"? In council wards with more than one elected representative, who is the representative who should take credit or blame for local services? Voters have more than one local representative and each could blame the other for not getting things done.

Coalitions can lead to instability

As we have seen, the majority of Scottish local authorities now have coalition administrations. City of Edinburgh Council has a ruling Scottish Liberal Democrat/SNP coalition. In August 2007, the new coalition announced a series of school closures. The decision was very unpopular and led to demonstrations and other protests by parent and pupil pressure groups.

The coalition claimed that long-term budgetary problems meant "rationalisation" of schools was required. As a result of the political pressure, the SNP group withdrew its support for the closures, without discussing this with their Scottish Liberal Democrat partners.

The coalition is now very strained. Edinburgh schools threatened with closure have been given a "stay of execution" until another review is carried out. Instability? Uncertainty? Confusion? These are precisely the criticisms that have been levelled at STV by supporters of FPTP of STV for years. Coalition governments are great when the parties agree with each other, but not so great when they fall out.

Activities

- Why was STV introduced in 2007 for elections to Scottish local authorities?
- In what ways has the introduction of STV changed the political complexion of Scottish local authorities?
- Find out the political complexion of your local authority. Do you have coalition government? If so, which parties are members of the coalition?
- Find out the elected councillors for your local authority ward.
- Why does STV give voters more power?
- Why is STV good for smaller parties?
- Give an example of instability in government involving a coalition.
- Draw a large spider diagram of the key arguments for and against the STV. Give examples for each point on the diagram.

Chapter 10   Voting Behaviour

The Traditional Model

The traditional model of voting behaviour was set out by the political scientist Peter Pulzer. His 1968 work famously concluded that social class was the major issue affecting voter behaviour. Everything else was "embellishment and detail".

But 1968 was a long time ago. Does social class still have this big an influence, or have other issues become more important?

Up until the 1970s there was a clear two party system. The Labour Party, with its close trade union ties, was widely seen as championing the working class. The Conservative Party, with its aristocratic leadership, represented the middle and upper classes. Elections, so the theory went, were decided by who could win over floating middle classes who had no long term loyalty to either party.

Social class as an influence on voting started to become more complex in the 1970s. According to political scientist Ivor Crewe, a new working class emerged: the C1 and the C2 classes. A process of so-called "voter de-alignment" began and continues to unravel to this day. Sometimes referred to as "Mondeo Man," this growing band of skilled workers from the C1 and C2 classes, rejected Labour's traditional "collectivist" approach to social policy.

Instead, they favoured an individual path to prosperity, choosing Conservative solutions. Economically, Conservative policies, such as the right to buy council housing, widen share ownership and lower taxes, appealed to voters who were, for the first time, enjoying the material wealth their parents had not.

Socially, they no longer worked in labour intensive industries, such as mining or car manufacturing, which encouraged trade unionism and values of collectivism. Instead, they worked in privatised industries where pay was dependent on performance, not the annual trade union negotiated salary. Many now owned their own business, as well as their home and their car.

The effect of these changes meant that the growing C1 and C2 classes now saw the world through privatised, individualist eyes, rather than those which emphasised working-class togetherness. Margaret Thatcher and the Conservatives championed these privatised values and duly collected the C1 and C2 vote.

The break up of the UK's old social class order explains the Labour party's move away from left wing, socialist policies, towards policies which value enterprise and individual responsibility.

New Labour and Social Class

New Labour may well have been launched by Tony Blair in 1994, but the birth of New Labour began a decade earlier, as Neil Kinnock drew the conclusion that Labour's traditional voters were now fewer and fewer in number.

According to Kinnock's "realists", Labour would have to reach out to the growing numbers of "have's" in British society, as well as the "have not's". Labour under Kinnock abandoned policies such as nationalisation and unilateral nuclear disarmament, and banished far left groups such as the Militant Tendency. By the mid-1990s, Labour had clawed its way back into contention for power. But, new leader Tony Blair felt the party had to send a powerful signal out to the middle classes that old Labour, which stood for socialism and state ownership, was gone.

In its place was "New Labour". For Tony Blair, New Labour would not be bound by "old-fashioned" ideas of social class solidarity. New Labour was about modernisation. It claimed to be neither old fashioned

Mondeo Man was a key demographic for New Labour

Left or Right, but "new and modern". New Labour sought to build a "big tent" of political support which could gather up supporters across the political divide and across social classes. Traditional Labour policies, such as a National Minimum Wage, would appeal to Labour's core support among the working class. At the same time, pledges not to raise income

107

tax appealed to middle class voters. Policies, such as tackling anti-social behaviour and cutting benefits for those not prepared to work, appealed to traditional Conservative voters.

Mondeo Man

At the heart of New Labour is an appeal to "middle Britain", or "Mondeo Man". The story goes, (and it may just be a story, no-one really knows how true this is) that Tony Blair was out in his Sedgefield constituency campaigning for Labour in the 1992 General Election.

Tony Blair, in those days a fairly unknown Labour MP, walked up a garden path where he met the owner of the house cleaning his new car, a Ford Mondeo.

Tony Blair asked the man if he intended to vote Labour. "No way" he exclaimed, puffing out his chest, "I'm voting Tory". Tony Blair could tell that he came from a working class background and he asked him why he wasn't voting Labour. He replied "I used to vote Labour, but now I'm successful. I've got a nice house. I go good holidays. I've got this new Ford Mondeo. Why would I want to vote Labour?"

Mondeo Man was important because he was part of a growing number of voters. He was also important because of where he lived. In the First Past The Post electoral system, voters of a similar social class tend to live next to each other. Predominantly working class areas tend to be safe Labour seats. By contrast, there are marginal seats, where a small swing in voting patterns can lose Labour a seat. The best example is Crawley in Sussex where, in 2005, Labour MP Laura Moffat won the constituency by just 37 votes from the challenging Conservatives.

All things being equal, Labour is unlikely to lose many safe, "working class" seats in a General Election. Likewise, the Conservatives should not lose too many of their safe "middle class" seats in the home counties of England. UK General Elections, therefore, are won or lost in the marginal seats. These are the seats where Mondeo Man, and his female counterparts "Worcester Woman" and "School Gate Mum", are to be found.

Indeed, thanks to the technology of the specialist software Mosaic, (Mosaic is similar to the information supermarket chains build up on us through loyalty cards), Labour has divided the population into highly precise social categories. The party's election literature is carefully scripted towards a diverse range of voters. "New-town materialists" are home-owning voters who like to earn and spend high wages. "Urban intellectuals" care about environmental issues and foreign affairs. Both are "middle England" targets for Labour's election strategists. By contrast, "white van culture", "rust belt resilience" and "older right-to-buy", refer to more socially conservative voters who have fears about job losses and immigration. Gordon Brown's 2007 Labour party conference soundbite, "British jobs for British people", was meant for both groups.

Gender

Party strategists are convinced that women hold the key to who wins and loses elections. Ever since the Second World War, women have made up the majority of Conservative voters. In fact, if it wasn't for female attachment to the Conservatives, Labour would probably have won every General Election since 1945.

In more recent times, women's votes have been up for grabs. It is middle class women who are sought after, though. Research, in both the United States and in Europe, shows that, once women become economically independent and/or receive a higher level of education, their political views move to the Left. The British Social Attitudes Survey found that a middle class, well-educated, well-paid woman with children under the age of 11, and working in the public sector, is 70% more likely to vote Labour than a similar man.

In 2005, women's votes were critical to Labour's success. According to MORI, 38% of

New Labour was built around Mondeo Man, Worcester Woman and School Gate Mum. Labour, for the first time in the party's history, won three General Elections in a row.

women voted Labour, 32% voted Conservative and 22% voted Liberal Democrat. By comparison, men voted equally for Labour and Conservatives (34%), with 23% voting Liberal Democrat. Whichever party wins the votes of School Gate Mum is likely to win the General Election. In 2005, if just women had voted, Labour would have won a Commons majority of 90, rather than 66. If just men had voted, Tony Blair would have had a majority of just 23 back-benchers.

"Worcester Woman" has become iconic in political terms, succeeding "Mondeo Man" as the key to Labour's election victories. Worcester lies in the heart of England, in the west Midlands. It is a marginal seat. The Conservatives would need to gain the parliamentary seat of Worcester at a General Election to have any prospect of becoming the largest party in the House of Commons.

All the parties are chasing the vote of Schoolgate Mum.

The online encyclopedia, Wikipedia, sums up Worcester Woman as "a white collar professional who worries about quality of life issues" and someone who would "previously have voted Conservative, but who swung to vote for Tony Blair's Labour Party".

Worcester Woman has a nice house. She will have a well-paid job. She will like spending money, but she works hard for it. She has a busy, stressful life. She has a mortgage and many demands on her time.

Middle-class voters such as Worcester Woman are not committed to any political party. They are classic floating voters. They will vote for whichever party can deliver economic prosperity, high quality public services and good law and order. Labour revamped all its policies and, crucially its image, to win the votes of the new middle classes.

School Gate Mum is the British version of the "Soccer Mums" found in the USA. They are working women who have demanding lives, balancing work and family responsibilities. Some psephologists have even broken down School Gate Mum into "Tailgate Mum" (the highly stressed urban driver) and, believe it or not, "Watercooler Mum" (she discusses social issues at her company's water machine).

School Gate Mum is not necessarily ideological. In fact, she does not see herself as political at all, and will rarely read the current affairs sections of newspapers, far less watch "heavy" news programmes. But she does care about the state of her community and the wider country. She will be interested in good childcare facilities. She will want good local schools. She will want a safe, happy community for her children to grow up in. School Gate Mum communicates with other School Gate Mums. She will discuss social issues at the school gate or in the office. She emails. She texts. She blogs and she networks. And she is very likely to vote. Every political party is chasing her!

New Labour was built around Mondeo Man, Worcester Woman and School Gate Mum. Clause 4 of the party's constitution was modernised. Out went "tax and spend". In came business-friendly Labour. Labour won the support of Rupert Murdoch's Sun newspaper and the Tory Daily Mail.

Labour, for the first time in the party's history, won three General Elections in a row. While Tony Blair has now gone, New Labour lives on. The New Labour "brand" may have been tainted by the Cash for Honours scandal and the war in Iraq. Gordon Brown is reluctant to use the term. But, Gordon Brown is as committed to the ideas of New Labour as Tony Blair was. Perhaps even more so.

Activities

- Why had Mondeo man turned towards the Conservatives?
- What did Mondeo man symbolise to Tony Blair?
- How did the Labour Party change to make itself more attractive to Mondeo Man?
- Why are women's votes so crucial to electoral success?
- Why is Worcester Woman so important to political parties?
- What political policies are likely to appeal to Worcester Woman?
- Why is School Gate Mum a key voter?

Core and Floating voters

Labour knows its core voters are working class and live in particular Labour heartlands. These are constituencies with large urban areas, especially those with council housing estates. Labour will not devote large amounts of party resources to campaigning in these constituencies. Party strategists believe the majority of voters in these constituencies will vote Labour. Here, the task is not one of persuading voters to vote Labour, but of motivating core voters to get out and vote.

Likewise, the Conservatives know their core vote lies within the private sector employed middle classes. Conservative core voters live in suburban areas, especially in the Southern Home Counties, which are within commuting distance to London. Like Labour, the Conservatives cannot take this voter for granted, but they know this voter is an instinctive Conservative and will not need much persuading. The Conservatives' task, similar to Labour, is to get its core vote out in the party's safe seats.

The Liberal Democrats know their core voter is based in the educated, quality newspaper reading, public sector working middle classes. Liberal Democrat core voters care about civil liberties, international affairs and want better public services and equal opportunities.

The SNP's core vote is mostly rural, in the North of Scotland. However, and since its transition to a modern, social democratic party which is slightly to the left of Labour, the SNP has started to make inroads into Labour's prized central belt heartlands.

Political parties are increasingly professional in their targeting of who and where their "core" and "floating" voters are.

Constituency 2005 General Election	% age Managerial/ Professional	Winning Party
Battersea	50.4	Labour
Kensington & Chelsea	50.3	Conservative
Wimbledon	50.0	Conservative
Richmond Park	49.9	Liberal Democrats
Hampstead & Highgate	49.2	Labour
Twickenham	47.6	Liberal Democrats
Hammersmith & Fulham	47.1	Conservative
Putney	46.7	Conservative
Cities of London & Westminster	45.8	Conservative
Tooting	45.2	Labour
UK	26.8	

Core voters are ideologically driven, even if they don't necessarily realise this. Core Labour voters feel Labour is their natural party, "for people like me". Core voters rarely discuss party policies. Their mind is made up. At the 2005 General Election, apathy was Labour's big worry.

Labour was not that concerned that significant numbers of its core voters would stray to the Conservatives or the Liberal Democrats, but that, perhaps due to the Iraq war or a dislike of Tony Blair, these voters would stay at home. Under this nightmare scenario, the Liberal Democrats would win sufficient Labour-held seats to allow Michael Howard's Conservatives to win.

To an extent this happened. Labour's parliamentary majority was cut from 167 to 66. But, Labour managed to win enough of both its core voters and floating voters in key marginal seats to win.

Because the FPTP voting system rewards parties with strong regional bases, there are many safe parliamentary seats. Therefore, it is the "swing" or marginal seats that will decide the outcome of the election. These are seats with significant numbers of middle class or "new" working class voters. These voters are not loyal to any single political party. Their vote "floats". They vote on issues. They weigh up their options. Which party will improve education and the NHS? Which party can lower my mortgage or make my house go up in value? Which party will tax me less or spend my taxes most wisely?

Codenamed "hardworking" or "aspirational families", these voters are to be found in marginal seats. They will be the subject of a great deal of attention from all the major political parties.

This has led to a new criticism of the FPTP voting system: that some voters are more influential than others. If you are middle class (more likely to vote and more likely to switch your vote) and live in a marginal seat (have a greater incentive to vote), your views will be listened to more than those of a poor person living in a deprived housing estate. Research shows that, if you lived in a marginal seat, you were around five times more likely to be contacted by parties in person or by phone, than if you lived in a safe seat.

Activities

- What are the main differences between core and floating voters?
- Why might core voters be disadvantaged by their political loyalty?
- Make a list of the characteristics of each political party's core voter.

Competing influences on voters

While voters have a social class and a gender based approach to politics, they are also members of other groups in society which can have an influence on voting behaviour. A middle class woman may have strong religious views (or not). Her ethnicity may play a big part in her attitude towards politics. Age can be a factor too.

So, the modern voter has a number of influences which compete with each other in determining how that person will vote. It is too simplistic to assume that working class voters vote Labour, without taking into account other long-term factors such as religion, race and age. In Chapter Eleven, we shall also analyse how short-term factors, such as the media and the party campaign, can influence voters.

Constituency 2005 General Election	% age Unemployed	Winning Party
Birmingham, Ladywood	18.7	Labour
Birmingham, Sparkbrook & Small Heath	13.8	Labour
Liverpool, Riverside	12.0	Labour
Birmingham, Hodge Hill	10.5	Labour
Tottenham	10.4	Labour
Manchester Central	9.8	Labour
Chamberwell & Peckham	9.6	Labour
Bethnal Green & Bow	9.4	Respect
Leeds Central	9.4	Labour
Hackney South & Shoreditch	9.3	Labour
UK	3.2	

Religion

Religion, in the past, was an issue in Scottish elections. The Conservative Party appealed to "Protestant" working-class voters, portraying Labour as the party of poor Catholic Irish immigrants. The influence of religion has declined in the post war years. Working-class Protestants have lost much of their "Britishness" and attachment to Conservatism. The latter part of the 20th century saw Labour dominate the Scottish political scene.

The SNP has, until recently, found it difficult to break Labour's support among Catholic West of Scotland voters who have been suspicious of an independent Scotland where Catholics would be a minority. In recent years the SNP has made a conscious effort to widen its appeal beyond its Northern heartlands. The party supports denominational schooling and an end to the Act of Settlement which bans Catholics from the British monarchy. In 2007, the SNP became the largest party in both Scottish Parliament and local government elections.

In the rest of the UK, new religious trends have been evident. Muslim voters used to be loyal Labour supporters. Michael Howard's "dog whistle" on immigration sent all the wrong signals out to Muslims, who sensed a racist undercurrent on immigration and an "Islamophobia" in the party's wider social agenda.

The war in Iraq, however, has damaged Labour's support among Muslims. At the 2005 General Election, George Galloway famously won the seat of Bethnal Green in London, with its large Muslim community, away from leading Labour MP Oona King, who had supported the war.

Oona King's defeat at the 2005 General Election by George Galloway showed that while Labour retains the support of ethnic minorities, their support cannot be taken for granted Labour cannot take the votes of ethnic minorities for granted.

blacks and Asian voters still more likely to live in poorer inner city areas and have lower income. Social class on its own however does not explain black and Asian support for Labour. There are now many professional, affluent British born black and Asian voters who may not necessarily identify with Labour.

Political geography plays a part. Many black and Asian voters are geographically concentrated. Some of these constituencies have become safe Labour seats, thus enabling a bond to be forged between Labour MPs and these communities. At the 2005 General Election, 15 black and Asian MPs were elected. 12 of these are Labour MPs.

Constituency 2005 General Election	% age Muslim	Winning Party
Birmingham, Sparkbrook & Small Heath	48.8	Labour
Bethnal Green & Bow	39.2	Respect
Bradford West	37.6	Labour
East Ham	29.7	Labour
Birmingham, Ladywood	29.5	Labour
Blackburn	25.7	Labour
Poplar & Canning Town	25.4	Labour
West Ham	23.6	Labour
Bradford North	20.6	Labour
Ilford South	19.6	Labour
UK	2.8	

Activities

- Why has religion declined as an influence on voting behaviour?
- What evidence is there that religion can still be an influence on voting behaviour?

Race

Black and Asian voters are significantly more likely to be Labour supporters. This could be a reflection of the social class relationship, with

However, Oona King's loss of the Bethnal Green and Bow constituency to George Galloway's Respect Party shows that race is not the only issue which influences the voting behaviour of ethnic minorities in the UK. Labour cannot take the support of ethnic minorities for granted. Race is, of course, sometimes closely associated with religion.

In 2005, Labour's share of the vote fell by more than the national average in each of the ten constituencies with the highest percentage Muslim populations. However, Labour still held nine of these seats. David Cameron's A-List of Conservative parliamentary candidates has placed black and Asian candidates in more winnable seats than in the past. The first minority ethnic member of the Scottish Parliament is the SNP's Bashir Ahmad.

> Activities
>
> • What evidence is there that race can play a part in voting behaviour?
> • Why can Labour no longer take the support of ethnic minorities for granted?

Age

For many years, older voters have been more likely to vote Conservative than younger voters. This is a generalisation. Age cuts across class, gender and racial categories too. However, in general, the older a voter is, the more likely he/she is to vote Conservative.

This may be due to the fact that voters in general tend to be wealthier as they get older. Traditional Conservative policies, such as tax cuts, may be more important to people with more to gain by cuts in tax. There may also be psychological reasons. In general, most people tend to become more conservative as they get older and less likely to favour radical change. Until the David Cameron era, the Conservative Party was an older party in terms of its membership and parliamentary candidates. The public perception of the party has been one of favouring support for "traditional" values, rather than supporting political or cultural change.

In 2005, the Conservatives won nine of the ten seats with the highest proportion of residents aged 65 and

over. By contrast, the Liberal Democrats performed better than their national average in constituencies with larger student populations. This may have been due to Liberal Democrat policies on, for example, university tuition fees, or the party's opposition to the war in Iraq which has been less popular among younger voters.

Constituency 2005 General Election	% age over 65	Winning Party
Christchurch	29.9	Conservative
East Devon	28.9	Conservative
Harwich	28.2	Conservative
Worthing West	28.1	Conservative
Bexhill & Bettle	28.0	Conservative
New Forest West	27.8	Conservative
North Norfolk	25.4	Liberal Democrat
Eastbourne	25.4	Conservative
West Dorset	24.6	Conservative
Bognor Regis Littlehampton	24.4	Conservative
UK	16.0	

Chapter 11: The Shaping of Political Attitudes

Impact of the Media

The relationship between the media and voter is a complex one. For example, the Sun switched its support from Conservative to Labour in 1997. Labour won a famous landslide victory in 1997. Does this mean "it woz the Sun wot won it", or does it mean that The Sun, like everyone else, saw which way the tide was turning and jumped ship to support the winning team?

Television and radio are part of the media. There are strict rules on political balance and political neutrality which the broadcasting media must follow. This has not stopped politicians and academics claiming that there is conscious, or even unconscious, bias shown on current affairs programmes. Some Conservative politicians claim that there is a "liberal" bias within the BBC and on Channel 4. Some academics have studied the language used and choice of interviewees on news and current affairs programmes and claimed that there is a "conservative" (with a small c) bias. Whatever the merits of these accusations, the broadcasting media is not allowed to show favouritism towards any one political party or set of ideological values. The print media of privately-owned newspapers is different.

Political parties like to have their good communicators to the fore in election campaigns. Labour's Alan Johnston can be relied upon to perform well in front of the cameras.

Newspaper support is very important to politicians. Tony Blair would not be so keen to have friendly relations with Rupert Murdoch (owner of BskyB and The Sun) if the media had no influence. Rupert Murdoch has been described as "the hidden member of Tony Blair's Cabinet". Former Labour leader Neil Kinnock was convinced that The Sun's tormenting of him cost Labour the 1992 General Election.

Kinnock urged Blair to get The Sun on Labour's side. But getting The Sun's support wouldn't, on its own, persuade voters to switch to Labour. The Sun's influence was its threat of campaigning against Labour. Tony Blair, it is argued, was so afraid of The Sun embarking on a campaign against, for example, the UK joining the Euro that he backed off having a referendum on the issue. According to Lance Price, Tony Blair's former Director of Communications, the Prime Minister was always looking over his shoulder to see what The Sun's headlines on asylum seekers or rising crime figures would be. David Clark, a special adviser to the late Robin Cook, said "I always took the view that Tony Blair's real Europe Minister was Trevor Kavanagh, the Sun's political editor".

Political parties would not spend so much time and energy on "spin", if what people see on television and read in newspapers had no influence on how they vote. It is the nature of that influence that is the key issue. Does the media shape people's beliefs? Or does it merely reinforce existing beliefs? Or, can it alone change people's ideas?

Professional spin doctors, such as Labour's Alastair Campbell, have manipulated the tabloid media. Party strategists keep "off-message" politicians or maverick candidates well away from the media. Instead, good communicators, and politicians seen to be popular with the voters, are pushed to the fore by the parties. Nowadays, most MPs and candidates are disciplined and prepared for media "lines of attack". Pagers and Blackberry mobile phones keep candidates up to date with the latest "line" from Party HQ.

The media rarely catches a politician off guard in modern elections. The exception occurred in 2001, when Labour's John Prescott punched a protestor who had thrown an egg at him. But did The Sun's "Two Jabs" headline really do him, or the Labour Party, any electoral damage?

Some voters may have thought "I'm not voting for that thug," but others may have thought, "I like that guy, he's not one of the usual boring politicians". It sums up the nature of this topic. We cannot really know for sure what the influence of the media is to any individual voter.

Activities

- In what ways do the broadcasting media report political events differently from the privately owned print media?
- What steps have the political parties taken to manage the print media's message?

Newspapers and their influence: a complex issue

Do Sun readers really vote according to what the paper tells them? Are not most Daily Mail and Daily Telegraph readers Conservative voters anyway? Likewise, surely most Guardian readers are Labour or Liberal Democrat supporters and that is why they buy the newspaper? Especially now that there are no longer big ideological differences between the main political parties, do newspapers really need to lecture their readers on who to vote for?

Things may have been different in the 1980s, when Labour had a socialist agenda and the Conservatives a tax cutting, privatising approach. But, these days, in the era of "big tent" politics and celebrity, what value is there in newspapers running highly partisan political campaigns? The business of newspapers is, after all, to sell newspapers. A newspaper, which bores, or worse, offends the viewpoints of its readers will not sell. Eighteen years after the Hillsborough disaster, The Sun's sales in the Merseyside area have not recovered from its branding of Liverpool football fans as thieves.

The Scottish Sun strongly opposed the SNP on election day 2007.

Newspapers will take a political "line", when it thinks this will be popular with its readers. This could be on an issue such as immigration, where right wing newspapers such as the Daily Mail and the Daily Express regularly have sensationalist front pages and editorials. But, in an era where the major political parties broadly agree on the big issues, and voters are much more likely to switch parties, it is unlikely that newspapers will be as unconditionally partisan in their support for a favoured political party as they were in the past. So, in this respect, it is the voters who influence newspapers and not the other way around.

Modern politics is all about building coalitions. The Sun wouldn't back any party that had not first captured its millions of readers, and wasn't therefore likely to succeed; it doesn't make winners, it adopts them

On the other hand, newspapers have a finely attuned awareness of the social class, age, gender and race of their readers. For example, the Daily Record will be very aware that, per head of the population, it sells more copies in working-class Drumchapel than it does in neighbouring, middle-class Bearsden. It would like to sell more copies in Bearsden, but caught in a circulation war with The Sun, its priority is to keep its existing readers, rather than seeking out new ones. The Daily Record and The Sun build their "political" message around what they believe their social class core wants to read. In this particular battle, party politics comes a long way behind football and celebrity gossip in column inches.

The quality press, for example, The Guardian, Independent, Herald, and Times know that their readership has certain geographical and social class based identities. Articles will be written which appeal to their readers' tastes and values. The quality press often support a political party. But, this support is rarely unconditional. Even the Daily Telegraph, a traditional Conservative newspaper, will have qualified support for Gordon Brown (something which demonstrates the scope of New Labour's big tent across the political spectrum). The quality press's support is much less overtly biased. It is usually more balanced and accepts that no one political party has all the answers. Their readers are highly educated and will resent being patronised by simplistic headlines.

So, there are certain undeniable facts about the media's influence on voters. The relationship is complex. Politicians are aware that the media has an influence, and they actively try to win its support. What that influence is, though, is hard to define. It is much more likely to be "drip, drip", than the result of a one-off buy. Rather than overtly promoting a political party, newspaper support for particular issues, such as immigration or tax cuts, may well influence readers to vote in a certain direction if political parties can successfully tap into the mood of voters.

It would be foolish to dismiss the media's influence. Isolating the influence of the media from all the other influences i.e. social class, gender, age, race, is notoriously difficult. Back in 1992, Neil Kinnock may have protested too much that the Sun lost him the election. Likewise, in 1997, The Sun may have protested too much that it won it for Labour. However, Tony Blair was so wary of the power of the tabloids to influence public opinion that he actively courted The Sun's support and drew away from making policies The Sun would not like. We cannot guarantee that The Sun would have swayed voters, but the possibility that it could, affected decision making in government.

Activities

- Why are today's newspapers less likely to be support a political party in an unconditional partisan way?
- How does coverage of political issues in the red tops differ from that of the quality press?
- Why is it difficult to assess the impact of the media on voting behaviour?

The media in the digital age

Too often the media is spoken about as if there is a single entity called "the media", with a simple, consistent party-political message which it transmits day-in, day-out to a gullible public. In reality, the media is composed of hundreds of newspapers, local and national. The media today is also hundreds of radio stations all over the country. It is 24/7 television and millions of websites and blogs. Staffing all these media are a huge range of individuals, with a diverse set of political opinions. The idea that one person, even a person as powerful as Rupert Murdoch, can control the views of all these people, day-in, day-out, is a bit simplistic.

What makes the digital media different from the "old media" is its interactivity. Newspapers traditionally had a letters page where readers could interact with each other. This took time, energy and commitment. In the digital age, rather than the voter being a passive consumer, the voter, it could be argued, is now in control. Online versions of newspapers allow readers to interact instantly, commenting on articles and stories. Readers can comment on stories online, quickly and effectively. The internet and new media such as You Tube are now allowing voters and political activists to use the media for their own political purposes.

One SNP supporter succeeded in creating a parody of Jack McConnell's soundbite of Scotland as "the best wee country in the world". The video clip, "the best wee numpty in the world", was a scathing attack on the personality of Jack McConnell and was forwarded by email to thousands of voters around the country. What influence did it have? Again, we cannot know for certain.

But a major part of the SNP strategy was its "Presidential" presentation of Alex Salmond as the best candidate for First Minister. The party even entered "Alex Salmond for First Minister" on the Scottish Parliament regional ballot paper, instead of the names of the party's list candidates.

Attacking Jack McConnell, however cruelly or unfairly, complemented the party's overall message. The best wee numpty video clip got third person email recommendation. Forwarded on and on, it "went viral".

Such video saboteuring has become a feature of American politics. It is likely that, with the growth of online networks such as Bebo and Facebook, digital campaigning is a new way of influencing voters.

Activities

- What differences are there between the digital media and the "old media"?
- What impact has the digital media had on elections?
- How could online social networks, such as Facebook, influence election campaigns?

The Party Campaign

Modern political parties accept that it is their job to "set the agenda" during election campaigns. Core voters need to be mobilised and motivated. Floating voters need to be wooed. The media needs to be "managed". The management of a party's election campaign is critical to its success.

In the 1980s, the Conservatives were the best-managed of the major political parties. They had a clear, tax-cutting message. They had professional media managers, the PR firm Saatchi and Saatchi. They ruthlessly exploited Labour's poor party organisation and public image. Tony Blair learned many lessons from these years. In 1997, Labour's "things can only get better" soundbite was simple and in tune with public dissatisfaction with the Conservatives.

However, the 2007 Scottish elections saw Scottish Labour run a dishevelled campaign which enabled the SNP to "set the agenda". In an internal party memo, Adrian Colwell, one of Jack McConnell's senior advisers, criticised the "negativity" of the Labour campaign. "We focused almost exclusively on attack and did not present or defend our record. We did not suggest momentum, that Scotland was becoming a better place. In contrast, the SNP offered the hope for something better." In addition, "the national organisation was hampered by in-fighting over who was in control, while local organisation was patchy".

The SNP had, in the past, run poor campaigns. The 2003 "Penny for Scotland" campaign, which

> "We focused almost exclusively on attack and did not present or defend our record. We did not suggest momentum, that Scotland was becoming a better place. In contrast, the SNP offered the hope for something better." Adrian Colwell, Senior Adviser to Scottish Labour, 2007

proposed an increase in income tax, was a vote loser. Until recently, the SNP did not have the funds to compete with the UK parties. This changed in 2007. Millionaire bus tycoon, Brian Souter, donated £500,000. Sir Sean Connery donated too. The SNP spent this money wisely. The party's message and its "brand" was a positive one. It did not go into detailed policy commitments which other parties could attack. It did not promise to increase tax, indeed the party's proposal to abolish Council Tax was spun in a way that offered tax cuts to key groups of voters – middle income voters and the elderly.

The SNP knew that Scottish voters were not completely convinced about independence, the very reason for the SNP's existence. So the party calmed these fears by promising a "try before you buy" option of a referendum on the issue if the SNP were elected. The slogan, "It's Time", was positive and unthreatening. This contrasted with Scottish Labour's approach which was, as the party admits, overwhelmingly negative. It was, however, supported by Scotland's tabloids.

Perhaps in an analysis of the influence of media impact on voting, it should be remembered that the SNP became the largest party in Scottish politics, despite being opposed by Scotland's two biggest newspapers, The Sun and the Daily Record. In response, the SNP blitzed the internet. The SNP website was redesigned by party Chief Executive Peter Murrell: "The new website no longer represents a passive information source; it is at the heart of a call to action".

Murrell used the website to promote the party's online petitions to stop the closure of Accident and Emergency wards and end student debt. The facility to add email addresses of friends provided the SNP with sympathetic contacts to launch future campaigns. "The website is all about bringing people to a community, around a flagpole – getting them to come through our website to back certain campaigns, which then hopefully persuades them to vote SNP". In the last week of the party's old website, only 120 people did more than just look at the home page. In the first week of the new one, the number jumped to 12,800. They were either joining petitions, emailing friends or making donations. The SNP took in £6000 in the first week.

The SNP promoted its biggest asset – Alex Salmond.

In modern elections, the personality of the leader appears to have assumed a new importance. Alex Salmond is widely acknowledged to be a shrewd and capable leader. He is a political heavyweight who has wide public recognition and respect. According to opinion polls, Alex Salmond is well liked by voters, more so than the SNP itself.

In the 2007 Scottish elections, Alex Salmond appeared everywhere. He had a weekly appearance on You Tube. His podcast could be downloaded from the home page of the party website. Alex Salmond beamed from all SNP election leaflets, bill boards and election broadcasts.

The party cheekily inserted "Alex Salmond for First Minister" at the top of the "list" ballot paper, gaining top billing due to its alphabetical content. Such psychological victories can make a difference. First Minister Jack McConnell fought hard, but he was hampered by disunity within Scottish and UK Labour parties and general confusion over the party's message. Stop the SNP yes, but what for?

Activities

- How can political parties be pro active in managing the messages portrayed by the media?
- What mistakes did Scottish Labour make in the 2007 Scottish elections?
- Give examples of how the SNP ran an effective, modern election campaign in the 2007 Scottish elections.

Trends in voter turout

There is a general feeling in the UK, and also the USA, that the political process is in something of a crisis. Media portrayal of politicians and governments is negative. Opinion polls show increasing apathy towards the political process. Rather than voting in elections, the public appear to be keener to participate via pressure groups or petition signing. Only 2% of UK citizens are members of political parties, down from 10% in the 1950s. There is a long-term decline in numbers of people voting, many see this as a sign of a growing disconnection between the public and politicians.

Is FPTP to blame?

Some people blame our current First Past the Post voting system (FPTP). Under FPTP there are many safe seats, where it is highly improbable that the incumbent candidate will lose. If you wish to vote for an alternative candidate, why bother? By contrast, there are around 10% of seats where there is a genuine challenge and the election is in doubt. Hence, only a very small number of voters actually have the power to change governments. That means that many millions of other voters are largely irrelevant to the outcome of the election. So it is hardly surprising if they don't feel terribly excited at the opportunity to vote.

Would PR make a difference to voter turnout?

It is claimed that different systems, such as the Additional Member System (AMS) will encourage people to vote. There was a high(er) turnout for the 1999 Scottish election (still not high), but since then Scottish voters have not turned out in high numbers. Likewise, STV, in Scotland at least, has not, on its own, produced greater turnouts. It has been argued by supporters of electoral reform, that people are discouraged from voting by the safe seats which are often a result of FPTP. However, turnout for 1999 FPTP local elections was higher than in 2007 under STV.

Turnout Scottish Parliament Elections 2007

Highest Turnout	%	Lowest Turnout	%
Eastwood	63.38	Glasgow	33.43
Western Isles	61.79	Glasgow Maryhill	35.96
Stirling	61.71	Glasgow Springburn	37.46
Strathkelvin & Bearsden	60.6	Glasgow Baillieston	39.83
Edinburgh Pentlands	59.37	Glasgow Pollok	41.15
Argyll & Bute	58.94	Glasgow Kelvin	42.65
West Renfrewshire	58.34	Glasgow Cathcart	45.29
Edinburgh West	58.08	Aberdeen Central	45.33
Galloway & Upper Nitsdale	57.66	Glasgow Govan	45.40

Some voters vote more often than others

So, if it is not the voting systems, why are voters not voting? Younger people, men, ethnic minorities, disabled and poorer people are less likely to vote than their older, female, white, non-disabled and well-off counterparts. In the 2007 Scottish Parliament elections, the gap between rich and poor in participation rates widened; turnout on the constituency vote reached 62% in the Western Isles (up more than three points on 2003) and 63.4% in Eastwood (up 5.4% on 2003). In Glasgow Shettleston, the Scottish Parliament's safest seat (coincidence?), turnout was just 33.4%.

People are living increasingly busy lives with growing work and family commitments. Having to go to an old school or church hall to vote is difficult to fit into the day. The younger generations, who vote even less than the rest, it is argued live their life through the digital world of mobiles and internet. It is claimed that they would vote more if voting could be done in this way, rather than the time consuming and "boring" method of using a grubby old pencil in the local primary school.

However, there remain great concerns over the security and integrity of online and text voting. In 2007, both ITV and BBC were forced to take action after scandals affecting phone in voting, including, of all places, Blue Peter!

Perhaps the answer lies in the quality of our political culture. The public, it seems, are switched off from mainstream politics. Yet parties outside of the mainstream do not attract much public support either. It is easy to criticise the quality of elected representative we have. But, few people are prepared to stand against these politicians themselves. Ultimately, in a democracy, do we not get the politicians we deserve?

Activities

- Why might the First Past the Post voting system lead to a decline in voter turnout?
- Why might a proportional voting system lead to greater turnouts?
- Why might proportional systems make no real difference to turnouts?

Acknowledgements

I am greatly indebted to the following people for their expertise, support and patience in the writing and publication of this book;

Lis and Joe. For Everything. Don't Stop Believin'

Linda Bruce, Zoe Brydon, Anna Campbell, Roseanna Cunningham MSP, Kathryn Daniels, Barry Graham, Ian Jack, Andy Kerr MSP, Raymond Kirk, Rory Mair, David Mundell MP, Kevin McGuckien, Veena Machanda, Jeff Maguire, James Newman, William Paul, Frank and Betty Petrie, Willie Rennie MP, Sandy Valentine, William Walker, Seonaid Whitley.

Kenny Dick and Paul Sheriff at Woods of Perth.

Online support: Neil Williams of LimaKilo Information Systems www.limakilo.com
IT solutions: Mark Newman of www.computer2computer.com
Design Genius: Heather Miller of www.golocalmag.com
Distribution King: Gordon Thomson at Aberdour Post Office
Transport Tsar: Trevor Francis at Aberdour train station.
Emergency catering: Lonies the bakers, High Street, Aberdour.

Please visit www.modernityeducation.co.uk to see the full range of products we have to support teaching and learning in Higher Modern Studies.

These include:

Web

www.modernityscotland.co.uk

The first and only website exclusively for Higher Modern Studies.

 Textbook

Success in Higher Modern Studies (with Pulse Publications)
ISBN 1 905817 02 9

A succinct and focused revision textbook for Higher Modern Studies, with model answers and marker comments for Paper 1 and Paper 2.

 Podcasts

To complement Modern UK Politics, ten mp3 files which enable students to revise at a time and place of convenience.

For teachers

We write a full Higher Prelim which assists Modern Studies departments with exam management and AIFL.

Powerpoints

All with teacher notes and hyperlinks.

Acknowledgements and thanks.

The author is grateful to the following for permission to use copyright images throughout the text:

The Scottish Government: p 4,13, 14, 15, 18, 21, 22, 25, 34, 47, 72, 83, 85, 89, 92, 103, 118. © Crown Copyright

The Scottish Parliament Corporate Body: Front Cover, p 5, 6, 7, 8, 9, 10, 15, 16, 28, 38, 59, 66, 76, 94, 102, 103, 116.
© Scottish Parliamentary copyright material is reproduced with the permission of the Queen's Printer for Scotland on behalf of the Scottish Parliamentary Body.

The House of Lords Information Service: p51, Lords Chamber: landscape
© Parliamentary copyright 2007
Photography by Deryc Sands.

The Conservative Party: p 62, 68, 74, 75, 80, 84, 91.

The Liberal Democrats: p20, 60, 70, 79, 88.
Photo library of the United Nations: p40 © UN Photo